W9-ADD-295

CONVERSATION ANALYSIS
The Study of
Talk-in-Interaction

GEORGE PSATHAS
Boston University

Qualitative Research Methods
Volume 35

SAGE PUBLICATIONS
International Educational and Professional Publisher
Thousand Oaks   London   New Delhi

For information address:

SAGE Publications, Inc.
2455 Teller Road
Thousand Oaks, California 91320

SAGE Publications Ltd.
6 Bonhill Street
London EC2A 4PU
United Kingdom

SAGE Publications India Pvt. Ltd.
M-32 Market
Greater Kailash I
New Delhi 110 048 India

Printed in the United States of America

Library of Congress Cataloging-in-Publication Data

Psathas, George.
    Conversation analysis: the study of talk-in-interaction / George Psathas.
        p.   cm. — (Qualitative research methods; v. 35)
    Includes bibliographical references.
    ISBN 0-8039-5746-7. — ISBN 0-8039-5747-5 (pbk.)
    1. Conversation analysis.   I. Title.   II. Series.
P95.45.P77   1995
302.3'46—dc20   94-33889

95 96 97 98 99 10 9 8 7 6 5 4 3 2 1

Sage Project Editor: Susan McElroy

For Alexander, Nicholas, and Selena

CONTENTS

Series Editors' Introduction   vii

1. **The Study of Interaction**   1
   Introduction   1
   Conversation Analysis   2
   Early Developments and Precedents   3
   The Critique of Category Systems   8
   Limitations of Goffman's Approach   10
   Transcribing Interaction   11

2. **Discovering Sequences in Interaction**   13
   Extended Sequences   21

3. **Sequence and Structure in Interaction**   27
   Identification and Recognition in Telephone
      Conversation Openings   27
   Turn-Taking Organization in Conversation   34
   Compliments and Compliment Responses   39

4. **The Methodological Perspective of Conversation
   Analysis**   45

5. **Talk and Social Structure**   54
   Calls to Emergency   58
   Perspective Display Sequences   61

6. **Conclusion**   67

Appendix: Transcription Symbols   70

References   79

About the Author   85

SERIES EDITORS' INTRODUCTION

While conversation analysis (CA) is one of the most important recent innovations in modern social science, it has not been presented in a clear accessible manner for students and interested scholars. This book, written by George Psathas, who has been active in research on and teaching of conversational analysis for twenty plus years, does that.

Interest in systematic qualitative analysis of natural data, especially speech, has been growing. This interest is reflected in recent books by Manning, Atkinson, Riessman, and Feldman in this Sage series. Using speech, from segments to sentences, to larger chunks up to and including entire texts, linguistic approaches to qualitative analyses vary in their degree of formalization of method.

CA is among the most precise and systematic of sociolinguistic approaches and, as Psathas shows, it has a well-developed conceptual framework, transcription conventions, analytic practices, and traditions of theorizing. It bridges the gap between linguistics, social psychology, and sociology.

Conversation Analysis: The Study of Talk-in-Interaction should become a definitive source for conversation analysis. It is based on and refined as a result of Psathas's extensive classroom experience in teaching CA at both graduate and undergraduate levels over many years. It is brief, lucid, accessible, and rich with engaging and relevant examples. The exposition is clear and advances understanding in a nonjargonistic fashion. It should be a tool with wide use in the social sciences, applied policy sciences, and business.

—Peter K. Manning
John Van Maanen
Marc L. Miller

CONVERSATION ANALYSIS
The Study of Talk-in-Interaction

GEORGE PSATHAS
Boston University

1. THE STUDY OF INTERACTION

Introduction

Social interaction has long been a phenomenon of interest to students of social life. A major problem has been how to study interaction, discover the ways in which various social actions are organized, and describe and analyze these features, using the rigorous methods of science so that reproducible results could be obtained by others examining the same phenomena.

Conversation analysis, the study of talk-in-interaction, represents a methodological approach to the study of mundane social action that has achieved these desired results. It has developed rigorous, systematic procedures for studying social actions that also provide reproducible results.

It takes up the problem of studying social life in situ, in the most ordinary of settings, examining the most routine, everyday, naturally

1

occurring activities in their concrete details. Its basic position is that social actions are meaningful for those who produce them and that they have a natural organization that can be discovered and analyzed by close examination. Its interest is in finding the *machinery*, the *rules*, the *structures* that produce and constitute that orderliness. Such examination requires the avoidance of preformulated theoretical or conceptual categories and the adoption of an open-mindedness and a willingness to be led by the phenomena of study.

As a development in the social sciences, it is clear that the term *conversation analysis* is a misnomer. It is not conversation but *talk-in-interaction* that is the broader and more inclusive characterization of the phenomena of study. *Interaction analysis* would perhaps be an even more appropriate term because all aspects of interaction, nonverbal and nonvocal, are also amenable to study, but this would be to claim perhaps too vast a territory.

Perhaps the term *ethnomethodological interaction analysis* would provide an appropriate qualification of this approach and indicate more clearly its distinctiveness.

For the purpose of this book, because our aim is to provide an advanced introduction to an area of study and a distinctive methodology, we shall continue to use terms that are in current use: *conversation analysis* and the study of *talk-in-interaction*.

Conversation Analysis

Conversation analysis studies the order/organization/orderliness of social action, particularly those social actions that are located in everyday interaction, in discursive practices, in the sayings/tellings/doings of members of society.

Its basic assumptions are:

1. Order is a produced orderliness.
2. Order is produced by the parties in situ; that is, it is situated and occasioned.
3. The parties orient to that order themselves; that is, this order is not an analyst's conception, not the result of the use of some preformed or preformulated theoretical conceptions concerning what action should/ must/ought to be, or based on generalizing or summarizing statements about what action generally/frequently/often is.

4. Order is repeatable and recurrent.
5. The discovery, description, and analysis of that produced orderliness is the task of the analyst.
6. Issues of how frequently, how widely, or how often particular phenomena occur are to be set aside in the interest of discovering, describing, and analyzing the *structures,* the *machinery,* the *organized practices,* the *formal procedures,* the ways in which order is produced.
7. Structures of social action, once so discerned, can be described and analyzed in formal, that is, structural, organizational, logical, atopically contentless, consistent, and abstract, terms.

The ethnomethodological character of conversation analysis should be clear. Social actions in the world of everyday life are practical actions and are to be examined as ongoing practical accomplishments. The logic or organization of such actions is a practical logic, an achieved organization, locally produced, in situ, in the "there and then" and the "here and now."

In various ways, conversation analysis drew upon and grew out of developments in phenomenology, ethnomethodology, and ordinary language philosophy. As it continues to extend its range of studies, it has had implications for such fields as social psychology, communication, pragmatics, discourse analysis, sociolinguistics, and cognitive science, as well as the branch of study out of which it originally emerged and continues to reside: sociology.

Early Developments and Precedents

When the theoretical and methodological approach that came to be called conversation analysis was first developing in the late 1950s and early 1960s, there were numerous other approaches to the study of interaction that were drawing the attention of researchers.

Foremost among these was Bales's *Interaction Process Analysis* (Bales, 1950), a preformulated category system of 12 categories, which were to be used to classify interaction in process. In this system, as in other kinds of category systems, a unit act is defined; each act, identified by its originator and the target person to whom it is directed, is classified into one of the categories of the system; and the categories, because they are preformulated, provide a limited set of meanings into which every act is to be classified.

Bales's system, developed in the late 1940s and culminating in the publication of his book in 1950, envisaged a means of achieving a reliable methodology for capturing the details of interaction, formulating it as a "problem solving process." Bales brought subjects to a controlled laboratory setting, placed observers behind a one-way mirror, and used newly developed audiotape technologies to record lengthy sessions of meetings. Participants were asked to discuss a problem and come to some resolution. His approach was also used by others in field settings including ones in which married couples would be presented with a number of problems to resolve, their interaction recorded and later analyzed using the same system.

The hopes raised by this kind of category system development were that generic problem-solving processes could be captured consistently by a single well-trained observer in field settings as well as in the laboratory. Also possible would be frequency counts of relevant categories; the development of mathematical formulae utilizing combinations of several categories, which would enable comparisons of different groups; and the development and testing of hypotheses regarding interaction processes in group problem solving.

The approach represented by this type of category system was based on a number of assumptions:

1. Units of action could be prespecified.
2. A system of preformulated categories could capture the meaning of an act.
3. The category system could be inclusive and exhaustive; that is, every act could be classified as a unit of meaning within the system.
4. Interaction could be quantified by the reduction of action to units of meaning, as defined within the category system.

As category systems gained ascendancy in social psychological research, particularly as these studies turned to the laboratory and controlled conditions for observation and experimentation, alternative approaches were also developing that eventually called into question the basic assumptions of category systems.

These included the psychological ecology of researchers such as Barker (1951), who undertook to follow a young boy for an entire day as he lived his usual activities in everyday settings, and Barker and Wright (1955), whose aim was to discover the ecological distribution of naturally occurring actions in real-world settings. Their methods relied on direct observation by a trained researcher in the field using descriptions of behavior.

Other researchers had begun to use recorders in settings such as the consulting room. Pittenger, Hockett, and Danehy (1960) published a detailed transcript of an individual psychotherapy session and noted such features of speech as pronunciation, intonation, rate, volume, tone, and the location and duration of pauses. Single utterances, such as "May I smoke?" (spoken by the patient) were subject to extensive analysis for both their interactional import and their relevance for the therapeutic encounter.

William Soskin and Vera John (1963) experimented with wireless transmitters, which could monitor a young married couple in order to record their naturally occurring interaction as they moved about, even in such places as a rowboat on a lake. Recorders received the transmission, and transcriptions of their naturally occurring interaction could be produced.

Birdwhistell (1952, 1970) was developing the study of kinesics and a system for analyzing body movements at the most micro level that could also be used to examine interaction.

Reusch and Bateson (1951) were calling attention to the interactive and dynamic character of communication, to the mutual influences involved in the communicative situation, and to the need to focus on the varieties and patterns of systems of communication. They called attention to the need for empirical studies of particular communicative situations, such as the therapy session, and for the development of new theories of communication (Bateson, 1955, 1972).

Anthropologists, influenced by developments in linguistics, were developing new approaches to the study of communication and language in connection with ethnographic studies of cultures. Some of these approaches, named by various researchers as the *ethnography of communication* (Gumperz & Hymes, 1964), *formal semantic analysis* (Hammel, 1965), *transcultural studies in cognition* (Romney & D'Andrade, 1964), *ethnoscience* (Frake, 1964; Sturtevant, 1964), and the *new ethnography* (Goodenough, 1957; Sturtevant, 1964), focused on meanings-in-use; on how members of a particular culture perceive, define, and classify, that is, their natural classification systems; and on the discovery and analysis of their underlying components. More broadly, some sought to develop an anthropology that would investigate directly the use of language in contexts of situation so as to discern patterns proper to speech activity. . . . it is not linguistics but ethnography, not language but communication, which must provide the frame of reference within which the place of language in culture and society is to be described. (Hymes, 1964, p. 2)

Erving Goffman (1959), meanwhile, in the tradition of social anthropology, had conducted his dissertation research in the Shetland Islands, utilizing conventional observational methods (direct observation and field notes). Goffman provided rich and illuminating descriptions, as well as theoretical interpretations, sometimes using metaphors drawn from drama, for understanding ordinary everyday interactions.

Harold Garfinkel, who had been developing ethnomethodology, was teaching at UCLA, and an informal seminar in ethnomethodology was underway. This seminar included, among others, Egon Bittner, Craig MacAndrew, Edward Rose, and Harvey Sacks.

The confluence of some of these approaches occurred in the late 1950s and early 1960s at the University of California, Berkeley, when Harvey Sacks, Emanuel Schegloff, and David Sudnow became graduate students in the department of sociology. The chairman of the department, Herbert Blumer, had recently come from the University of Chicago and deliberately planned to focus on qualitative perspectives in sociology. Erving Goffman, whose degree was from Chicago, was hired to teach in the department.

As Sacks, Schegloff, and Sudnow worked with both Garfinkel and Goffman, a distinctive viewpoint began to emerge.

From Goffman, who at the time was lecturing on and writing what was to be published as *Behavior in Public Places* (1963), came the validation of an intense focus on naturally occurring activities as showing the promise of becoming a field in its own right. With the development of the portable tape recorder, the ways in which persons actually spoke and interacted became subject to even closer scrutiny and analysis. And with the development of ethnomethodology, influenced by the phenomenology of Schutz and the ordinary language philosophy of Wittgenstein, it would seem inevitable that radically new and different approaches to the study of everyday life would emerge.

Harvey Sacks, employed at the Suicide Research Center in Los Angeles, began to use the tape recorder to record telephone calls to the Center, recordings that provided him with a rich source of data. He began to examine such matters as opening lines in a telephone call to the Center, for example, "This is Mr. Smith may I help you." His concern was with how social actions are organized, how the parties in talk understand each other, and how the practical work of social life is accomplished. In examining such expressions as "no one to turn to" or "you want to find out if anybody really does care," Sacks was able to show how the relationship of the person to society was visibly demonstrated in their talk. He recorded and collected such empirical, naturally occurring interactional interchanges and lectured on them in his classes (Sacks, 1964-72). His lectures were tape-recorded, transcribed, and then circulated widely to colleagues or interested parties, and were finally edited and published in 1989 and 1992, many years after his tragic death in 1975.

Thus the tape recording technology served a dual function. In contrast to Goffman, who lectured in a more traditional fashion as he worked out ideas for later publication in his papers and books, Sacks tried to organize his lectures as coherent wholes, and analyzed recorded interactions collected from various everyday life settings.

Sacks's lectures demonstrated his methodology as well his theoretical orientation. For Sacks, these were inextricably linked. The mundane world required close examination on its own terms, not the use of a theoretical microscope fashioned out of abstract terminology or created in domains of study extrinsic to the phenomena being studied. Conceptualizations of the phenomena that generalized their properties and separated them from the contexts in which they occurred were not sought. In contrast to Goffman, whose prolific conceptualizations often dazzled the reader, Sacks's concern was to remain descriptively close to the phenomena and, if necessary, to use conceptualizations that retained their everyday intelligibility, for example, greetings, asking for a name, closings, openings, and the like; as well as to seek to describe these in formal analytic terms, for example, sequential structures, paired utterances, adjacency pairs, and the like.

It was in this sense that the early Sacks and other conversation analysts were achieving a science that was grounded in a descriptive phenomenology of the mundane world. Abstract and generalizing conceptualizations and theoretical formulations were avoided in order to first discover and analyze the natural organization of social actions.

Theoretical formulations drawn from sociology were considered "practical reasonings," whose very character might need to be studied rather than accepted as explanatory schemas. The methods of the social sciences were to be subjected to the same scrutiny and examination to discern their reflexive relation to the phenomena observed.

The Critique of Category Systems

A critique of category systems and, by implication, all efforts to classify and code units of interaction emerged from the developments in ethnomethodology and conversation analysis and was multifaceted (see also Cicourel, 1964).

1. Category systems, because they were *preformed* or *preformulated* in advance of the actual observation of interaction in a particular setting, would structure observations and produce results that were consistent only with their formulations, thereby obscuring or distorting the features of interactional phenomena.
2. They were *reductionistic* in seeking to simplify the observer's task by limiting the phenomena to a finite set of notated observables.
3. They *ignored the local context* as both relevant for and inextricably implicated in meaning production, and instead substituted the theoretical assumptions concerning "context and meaning," which were embedded in the category system itself.
4. They were *quantitatively biased* in that they were organized for the production of frequency counts of types of acts, and thereby were willing to sacrifice the understanding of locally situated meanings in order to achieve quantitative results.

The *produced* organization of findings about social actions based on category systems was therefore not a description and analysis of the *natural* organization of the activities. The conversation analysts were concerned with the *intrinsic orderliness of interactional phenomena* and assumed, as Sacks put it, that there was "order at all points." It remained for the analyst to discover that order, not impose an order on phenomena based on a preconceptualized category system.

This basic difference meant that interaction analysts who were influenced by ethnomethodology and conversation analysis soon had very little in common with those who were continuing to work in social psychology and sociology on the study of interaction. Certainly, the emphasis on naturally occurring interaction meant that laboratory experiments with artificially constructed groups were no longer necessary.

The tape recorder (and later the video recorder), which could be taken into the field or connected to a telephone, was capable of collecting numerous instances of interaction. In fact, data in vast amounts could be obtained in relatively short amounts of time, with minimal expenditure of funds, time, and other resources. The transcription and analysis of such data were to prove more challenging, however, and the question of *how* such materials would be analyzed emerged as the paramount concern.

The users of coding and category system methodologies had an easier time. They collected data in coded form and transformed these into various kinds of quantitative tabulations. Various formulas for rates and changes over time were remarkably simple to achieve, though ultimately the interpretation of findings remained just as difficult a task as it had always been.

In turn, conversation analysts were criticized for not having "enough" instances of any of the types of data collected, reported frequencies were "small and inadequate," and "sweeping interpretations" were considered to be based on micro incidents and single cases. The early criticisms of the conversation analysts were generally based on the assumptions and epistemological positions of those who favored coding and category systems and, in general, the development of quantitative modes of analysis.

In contrast to the coded category systems, Goffman's rich and illuminating descriptions of everyday interaction provided an important resource for the main position advanced by conversation analysts, namely, that it was possible to study everyday situations and to make important discoveries concerning how persons engaged in interaction. His approach was qualitative rather than quantitative and drew on a variety of methodologies, from social anthropology to animal ethology. He organized his observations, using new conceptual frameworks, and drew on terminology from other domains of study such as drama (Goffman, 1959), games (Goffman, 1963), and ethology (Goffman, 1971). He was able to show that important matters of great social significance resided in the everyday, ranging from how persons presented themselves to others, the social proprieties observed in face-to-face gatherings, the organization of traffic on public sidewalks, the ways in which persons claimed territories in public places, how they distanced themselves from role performances, how mental hospital residents achieved an underlife in total institutions, and so on. His range was enormous and his writings proliferated.

Goffman's numerous writings increasingly attracted attention and enhanced the visibility of his descriptive and qualitative perspective. Nevertheless his approach resonated with functional, normative, and structural interpretations of social organization.

Goffman's was also a critical voice from within the body of the discipline that sought to redirect it to "neglected topics" by providing examples of how this could be done. He showed that description and analysis, without hypothesis testing and reductionistic operational definitions, could contribute to understanding social processes and structures. He defied orthodox approaches; criticized methodologists in the social sciences by ignoring them; and avoided such issues as sampling, statistical analysis, research design, and the like. (Once he quipped that laboratory social psychologists were too busy playing with their equipment to see what was happening in front of them.)

Although he influenced the early development of conversation analysis, the two perspectives did not merge. Goffman, in an important sense, provided legitimacy for the study of the details of everyday interaction. But, where the conversation analysts immediately adopted the technology of the tape recorder and video, Goffman eschewed both. In the rich variety of his examples and illustrations, virtually none are transcripts of recorded interactions (the major exception is his essay "Radio Talk," 1981b). He continued to rely on observations, field notes, excerpted material from the reports of others, including journalists, novelists, and playwrights, and even hypothetically constructed examples to illustrate his conceptualizations.

The "field" he opened for direct study was that of situated co-presence, the everyday occasions when persons were physically in each others' presence, aware of and interacting with each other, involved in ongoing social relationships, face-to-face. This has been referred to variously as the *situated activity system, face-engagements, encounters* or *focused encounters*, and in his last writings as "the interaction order."

Limitations of Goffman's Approach

From the perspective of ethnomethodology and conversation analysis, Goffman's approach appeared to be inadequate for achieving a social science of social actions, a science based on actual empirical occurrences of interaction between and among persons in everyday social situations. Such a science would have a rigorous method, one that could be taught to others, and, because it would be based on collected empirical instances of interactional phenomena, could provide for replicable results. By not adopting theoretical conceptualizations in advance of any study, it would be feasible to remain as completely true to the phenomena of study as possible. By eschewing the development of abstract theories that aimed to gloss variations in the interest of achieving broad scale generality, this approach also proposed to present its results and findings in terms that would be distinct from prevailing theoretical perspectives in the social sciences.

Although Goffman also did not try to connect his theoretical conceptualizations to prevailing theoretical perspectives, he did move toward more abstract and general concepts, which glossed over the very situational particulars that had originally been the focus of his inquiry.

He maintained an interest in formulations that emphasized the ritual, the moral, the normative, and the structural aspects of social activities.

Goffman remained conversant with the developments in conversation analysis but maintained a critical dialogue with it in his writings. (See especially his allusions in *Relations in Public*, 1971, and *Forms of Talk*, 1981a.) When he studied the same kinds of interactional phenomena as the conversation analysts, he introduced his own conceptualizations (e.g., "couplets" rather than "adjacency pairs") and consistently tried to connect the observation of the so-called micro-order to so-called social structural or functional issues. In this respect, his orientation to the normative order persisted throughout his lifetime of writings.

In contrast, the conversation analysts (and the ethnomethodologists) persisted in examining order as a produced and achieved matter, something to be studied in the various ways that this achievement was accomplished in and through the activities of members of society. They remained indifferent to various broad scale conceptualizations and general theories, in the interest of studying interaction itself and discovering and describing its orderliness.

Transcribing Interaction

Because it was necessary to describe the details of interaction in order to provide both the researcher and the reader with sufficient information to understand exactly not only what but *how* the persons were speaking, a system of symbolic notations that could be used in transcribing interaction evolved. This system of transcription basically tries to preserve some of the key features of talk, namely certain kinds of intonation, pauses, sound stretches, emphasis, and the like. The development and use of such symbols was related to the kinds of interactional phenomena being studied and therefore, as new topics were studied, additions were made to the notation system. Over a period of time, most researchers settled on the transcription notations developed originally by Gail Jefferson.

A commonly used system of transcription symbols is also necessary to facilitate the communication and understanding of research studies. Those doing conversation analysis and presenting their findings are expected to provide detailed transcripts of their data. The use of varying and inconsistent notation systems could possibly confuse rather than enhance communication, and would not be conducive to the cumulation of findings concerning the same phenomena.

The full details of the system are presented in the Appendix, but certain key features, which will facilitate the reading of transcripts in the next chapters of this book, are minimally the following:

Emphasis is noted by underlining or using italics for those parts of an utterance that are stressed.

Sounds that are stretched are indicated by colons, ::::::, for example, so::::

Sounds that are cut off are marked by a dash, for example, la- bu-

Pauses may be noted by timings in seconds and tenths of a second (e.g., 1.2), with micro pauses of less than two tenths of a second by a dot (.).

Brackets ([ ) indicate speech that is overlapped.

Punctuation is used to indicate features of speech such as pitch. For example, a question mark (?) indicates rising intonation, a comma (,) continuing intonation, and a period (.) terminal falling intonation.

2. DISCOVERING SEQUENCES IN INTERACTION

The discovery of a turn-by-turn sequential organization of interaction was one of the first important discoveries and foci of attention in the development of conversation analysis.

As Harvey Sacks, in his work at the Suicide Prevention Center in Los Angeles, began to analyze audiotape recordings of calls to the Center, he noticed certain recurrent phenomena that appeared in sequences of talk. Persons who called would often not give their names, whereas the Center wished to obtain a name and wanted to be able to increase their chances of doing so.

Sacks noticed that very early in the conversation there were indications of possible difficulties in obtaining the caller's name. He examined sequences between the answerer, generally a social worker, and the caller, such as the following:

(1)
Answerer: This is Mr. Smith may I help you
Caller: Yes, this is Mr. Brown
(2)
Answerer: This is Mr. Smith may I help you
Caller: I can't hear you
A: This is Mr. <u>Smith</u>.
C: Smith

He began to speak of such phenomena as found in example 1 as "asking for a name without asking" and noted that the caller provided a name without being asked directly; whereas in example 2, the caller did not.

He found that instances such as example 2 signaled difficulty in obtaining a caller's name and it appeared as though callers were refusing to give a name, although not asked directly to do so.

He noticed that what speakers do in their next turns is related to what prior speakers do in the immediate prior turn. Exchanges occur as *units*, as in the following example of a Greeting-Return greeting exchange.

(3)

  A: Hello
  B: Hello

The symmetry of these exchanges did not appear to be accidental, but was a recurrent feature of opening sequences. He first called these *pairs* and began to consider them as *units*. Sequential units could be examined as phenomena in their own right, to see how they were organized and to learn what they accomplished.

As units they seemed to be organized as follows: they were two turns in size; speaker change occurred such that one speaker produced the first turn and a second speaker produced the next; what occurred in the first part of the pair of utterances was relevant to what occurred in the second; and what occurred in the second part of the pair was related to what had occurred in the first.

He noticed that the utterance, "This is Mr. Smith may I help you," provides a "slot" for the caller to give their name. Because the answerer has also identified themselves with a particular form of address (title + last name), this form is offered as the one to be used by the caller.

When, in next turn, caller does not produce a self-identification, they have not taken up the form offered and thereby indicate that they may not wish to do so. However, it is possible, as example 2 indicates, to refuse to take up the offered form by instead asking for a repetition of the answerer's first utterance ("I can't hear you") and to focus instead on the matter of achieving clarity or understanding, rather than on the matter of providing their own name.

When Sacks noticed that these callers, later in the call, may refuse to provide a name when directly asked, and that a direct asking could also lead to requests by the caller for an account (or reasons) for the request, he was able to argue that the first opening exchange of "This is Mr. Smith may I help you" also was a way of asking for a name *without* having to provide an account (or reasons) for the asking.

Thus an utterance could be found to work in a number of ways. The work that the utterance accomplishes is not limited to one and only one meaning. The close examination of actual sequences, with attention to the contexts of their occurrence, was found to be particularly informative.

Sacks (1989, p. 29) was encouraged to believe that "naturally occurring social activities are subjectable to formal description" and that such description can "permit us to see non-trivial ways that actual activities in their details are simple." The implication was that "sociology can be a natural observational science" because it was demonstrable that social actions are "methodical occurrences." The description of social actions would thus be the "description of sets of formal procedures which members employ."

In this respect, conversation analysis has been consistently oriented to the discovery, description, and analysis of methodical occurrences, of the formal procedures that are used by members in accomplishing everyday social actions. Descriptions can achieve, in turn, a formal character, although the phenomena they describe are concrete, actual instances of mundane occurrences. That conversation analysis can and does produce formal descriptions has troubled some readers, who seem to expect that because it focuses on ordinary and concrete instances of interaction, it will produce descriptions that use the same vocabulary as everyday actors in the social scene. The confusion here is between formal description and vernacular characterizations of action. It is not the terms used that make a description formal, but the adequacy of the description for capturing, noting, and preserving the features of the organizational practices, the methodical procedures, that are being analyzed.

As Schegloff (1968, 1979) also found in collecting instances of telephone call openings, ranging from ordinary calls between friends to calls to disaster centers and businesses, opening sequences could be analyzed to reveal important organizational properties. In his examination of first turns, he noted what came to be called Summons-Answer sequences.

These involve a first turn in which a speaker calls for the attention and response of the other, and a next turn in which the other indicates that they have heard and are able to respond.

(4)
    A: Bill?
    B: What?
(5)
    A: Excuse me.
    B: Yes.

For the telephone call, the prototypical first turn Summons is the ringing of the phone, and the second turn the answering of the call or Answer to the Summons.

(6)
> (ring)
> A: Hello

Summons-Answer sequences, as found in empirical instances, were analyzed and noted to have a number of properties:

1. They are two turns in length.
2. First speaker produces the first pair part.
3. Second speaker produces the second pair part.
4. They occur at the beginning of interaction sequences.
5. They are nonterminal in that they do not end encounters.
6. The speaker who speaks the first part, the summons, is obliged to speak again (though deferral may be requested, as in "wait a minute," or a change of mind indicated, as in "oh never mind").
7. The answerer of the summons is obliged to listen, though availability to listen may be deferred (as in "just a moment").
8. They are nonrepeatable once an answer occurs.
9. They may be repeated if not answered.
10. They need not be verbal but could, for example, involve taps on the shoulder, hand waving, nods, head shakes, and so on.

The relation between the first pair part and the second pair part of this type of utterance was then proposed to be one of *conditional relevance*, and the structure itself was called *an adjacency pair*.

Other sequences that were identified and were found to have similar *structural or formal properties* included the following:

Greeting-Return Greeting
> A: Hi
> B: Hi

Question-Answer
> A: What are you doin?
> B: Nothin

Closings
> A: Bye dear
> B: Bye

Invitation-Accept/Decline

A:	Wanna go out tonight?	A:	Wanna go out tonight?
B:	Sure.	B:	Sorry, I'm busy.

Offer-Accept/Decline

A:	Want something to eat?	A:	Want something to eat?
B:	Sure, thanks.	B:	No, thanks

Complaint-Apology/Justification

A:	You're late for class.	A:	You're late for class.
B:	Oh, sorry.	B:	The traffic held me up.

This discovery of structure in interaction sequences proved to be an important finding because it confirmed what had been proposed in ethnomethodology from the outset, namely, that there is order to be found in the most mundane of interactions, and that close examination of actual occurrences would enable the analyst to discover, describe, and analyze that orderliness.

Order was seen to be a produced order, integral and internal (endogenous) to the local settings in which the interaction occurred. That is, it was ongoingly produced in and through the actions of the parties. It was not imposed on them, nor was it a matter of their following some sort of script or rules. They were freely involved in that production and were themselves oriented to that production. What they were doing was carrying out actions that were meaningful and consequential for them in that immediate context. They were, for example, opening up conversations, or closing them, or exchanging greetings, or responding to invitations, and so on.

The phenomena that were being studied were everyday social actions. Perhaps, if we were to call these topics of study the *organization of social actions*, their sociological import might be more readily understandable. Because they worked under the rubric of conversation analysis, their findings were labeled by many in sociology as the *study of language* or *sociolinguistics,* and therefore possibly belonging to some other discipline. Because the phenomena studied seemed to be restricted to *micro* sequences, they were often judged to be of little import to the understanding of *macro* social structures or processes. (More of this discussion later.)

Returning to our examination of one of the first basic structures discovered, that of adjacency pairs, the major dimensions of their organization can be delineated as follows:

1. They are (at least) two turns in length.
2. They have (at least) two parts.
3. The first pair part is produced by one speaker.
4. The second pair part is produced by another speaker.
5. The sequences are in immediate next turns.
6. The two parts are *relatively ordered* in that the first belongs to the class of first pair parts, and the second to the class of second pair parts.
7. The two are *discriminatively related* in that the pair type of which the first is a member is relevant to the selection among second pair parts.
8. The two parts are in a relation of *conditional relevance* such that the first sets up what may occur as a second, and the second depends on what has occurred as a first.

The "rule of operation" of such adjacency pairs is that if the first pair part is produced and so recognized by the speakers, then "on its completion the speaker should stop and next speaker should start and produce the second pair part from the pair of which the first is a recognized member" (Schegloff & Sacks, in Turner, 1974, p. 239).

The power of these kinds of structures in interaction can be found in such fundamental and recurring interactions as the openings and closings of interactional encounters. When a speaker produces the first pair of an adjacency type structure, they may constrain what next speaker may do in next turn. If next speaker is not to produce the appropriate next, they may have to show in some way why they do not do so, for example, a failure to understand, a nonhearing, a misunderstanding, or a disagreement. Because the first pair part implicates what is appropriate for the next turn, what occurs in the next turn is closely monitored for its relation to the first. Even slight pauses or hesitations can be indicative of some sort of interactional troubles.

The conventional and recurrently smooth operation of openings and closings such as "hello-hello" and "goodbye-goodbye" is indicative of members' recognition of their significance. Such adjacency pairs serve to facilitate interaction at key junctures and, by virtue of their conventionality, provide persons with ready-made methods for achieving specific outcomes.

As work proceeded, a number of *four*-part structures were also discovered. These operate in similar ways, but are four turns in length.

For example, invitations and their acceptance or decline can occur with presequences, or prefatory sequences, that are implicative for what follows.

(7)
    1. A: Are you busy tonight?
    2. B: No
    3. A: Wanna go to a movie?
    4. B: Sure

Here the two-part prefatory sequence in lines 1 and 2 represents a possible entry into the invitation, but is not the invitation itself. Depending on how B responds to the preinvitation, A can either proceed with the invitation or shift to a different topic. In this case, because the preinvitation is responded to with what A can understand as an availability on the part of B, A may proceed with the invitation proper.

Or, in closings (Button, 1990, p. 132):

(8)
    1. A: Oright
    2. B: Okay [honey
    3. A: [bye dear=
    4. B: =bye

Prior to the actual *termination* sequence in lines 3 and 4 that ends the conversation, the parties engage in a *preclosing* sequence. This preclosing is represented by a first turn offer to close by A, and an acceptance by B in second turn. This would indicate that there are no more topics to be introduced to the conversation and that both parties are ready to move to a terminal sequence.

Thus the four-part sequence has *two* ordered adjacency pair structures in which the first adjacency pair implicates what could be a relevant second adjacency pair.

It is obviously possible for the presequence not to flow into the next terminal one if either of the parties indicates a nonreadiness or interest in so doing by whatever they may say in third turn.

For example (Button, 1990, p. 137):

(9)
1. Geri: Oka:y
2. Shirley: Alright?
3. Geri: Mm.h [m̲:?
4. Shirley: [D'yih talk tih D̲ayna this week?
5. Geri: hhh Yeh.....

In this instance, after the first and second turns, which are preclosings, Geri does not initiate a *terminal* first pair part, but instead moves out of the closing sequence, a move that is taken up by Shirley, who then introduces another topic and the conversation continues.

The discovery and analysis of such structures as two- and four-part sequences proved to be important and significant. A search for additional such structures in conversational interaction was thereby initiated, a focus that appeared to some to be microscopic in its attention to the details of closely ordered sequences.

At the same time, there continued to be an interest in larger, more extended sequences, work on which had been begun early as evidenced in Sacks's lectures on such topics as stories and on the calls to the Suicide Prevention Center, where such phenomena as "refusing to give a name," "no one to turn to," I want to see if anybody really cares," and so on, had been analyzed.

The important point to note here is not that two- or four-part sequences became the topic of inquiry, but rather that social actions such as invitations or closing a conversation were found to be organized in this sequential fashion.

The significance of these discoveries should not be underestimated. For the first time in the study of social interaction, *sequential structures of actions* were discovered in naturally occurring situations. A new unit of interaction had been identified, one that was genuinely *inter*actional because it involved two persons, one speaking first and the other next, in close temporal order, in immediate turns. Adjacency pairs were of importance in this early work because their discovery demonstrated that members were attuned to the production of ordered sequences. This was not an analyst's construction. The meaning of the social action could not be understood without considering the sequence; that is, a first part was a first in relation to what happened in immediate next turn. To "understand the meaning" of what persons were doing required attention to the *sequences* of their actions. Two-part sequences were significant interactional phenomena because, among other things, the occurrence of a first (pair part) constrained what the other might do in a next turn or action. The nonoccurrence or absence of the conditionally relevant next (the second pair part) was noticeable by the parties, an absence that could result in attention to issues of nonhearing, nonunderstanding, misunderstanding, or to a repetition of the first, or a disruption in the continuity of the interaction, and so on. In other words, the consequences were nontrivial. The study of greetings and openings and closings thereby achieved considerable significance in conversation analysis, because these represented the first discoveries of orderly interactional phenomena whose methodical procedures, machinery, rules, or sequential structures could be demonstrated, analyzed, and formalized.

Extended Sequences

At the same time there continued to be an interest in longer, more extended sequences, such as "telling stories" in conversation, which showed that these sequences were also sequentially organized and fitted within the particular context of interaction. They were shown (Schenkein, 1978, p. 219) to have a

> story preface in which a teller projects a forthcoming story, a next turn in which a co-participant aligns himself as a story recipient, a next in which teller produces the story (a series of segments in which teller's talk can alternate with recipient's) and a next in which the story recipient talks by reference to the story. Further, the story preface can have consequences for the story's reception, and thus a rather extended series of turns at talk can be seen as a coherent conversational unit.

In further work, Schenkein (1978, pp. 219-220) noted how stories emerge from turn-by-turn talk, how they are locally occasioned by it, and how, upon their completion, turn-by-turn talk is reengaged. Stories thus are sequentially implicative for further talk.

With regard to its beginning, a story may be triggered by something said in the conversation, which may or may not be topically coherent with the talk in progress. By connecting the story to prior talk, storytellers propose that there is a relationship between the prior talk and the story, and that the story is therefore appropriate.

One such device that Schenkein notes for introducing a story into the talk is the use of a *disjunct marker* (e.g., "oh" or "incidentally," or "by the way"), which signals that what follows is not topically coherent with the prior talk. Another device is an *embedded repetition* in which some part of prior talk is mentioned, as in "speaking of X," where X is the repeated element. These methods serve to show that the story is not disconnected from the ongoing talk, but is in some ways continuous with it.

At the story's end, turn-by-turn talk may reemerge, and various methods may be used to show that there is a relationship between the story and subsequent talk. These serve to show not only that the story had sequential implications but also that it was appropriate to be told at just this place in the conversation. Schenkein demonstrates these devices from specific segments of actual recorded interaction. Additional work on storytelling in conversation, by Jefferson (1978) and Goodwin (1984) among others, has added to the understanding of how stories are accomplished in conversation.

Sacks (unpublished lectures of April 9 and April 16, 1970) had first noted the significance of the organization of storytelling in conversation:

> Since they take more than one utterance to produce, it is relevant that recipient learns (hears) that a story is to be produced. Otherwise, because of the turn-taking system of conversation, a speaker at a turn completion point may find that another person begins to speak. How is the other to know that it is not a place to speak since any next possible completion point is a place to speak. One way would be to produce an utterance which says that what I plan to say will take more than one utterance and that the number of utterances cannot be specified in advance. If this is accepted by the others, then the speaker may retain the right to speak over a series of utterances.

A *story preface*, Sacks proposes, is a way to do this. The story preface is an "utterance that asks for the right to produce extended talk and says that the talk will be interesting. . . . At the completion of that 'interest arouser' . . . one stops, and it's the business of others to indicate that it's okay and maybe also that they're interested, or it's not okay or they're not interested."

Another problem is how to tell when the story is over. The story preface may contain information that reveals what it will take for the story to be over. The hearer can then attend to the telling, to find the point at which this information occurs. If missed, the teller can point out that that point has now been reached.

With regard to the organization of the story

> hearer's business is not to be listening to a series of independent utterances, but to a series of sentences that have their connectedness built in so that their connectedness has (to be understood to understand any one of them). Coherence of the story (depends on) requiring that if you're going to understand it at the end, you've got to keep in mind what's been told earlier. (Sacks, unpublished lectures)

As another example of a study of extended sequences, we can consider work on direction-giving in interaction (Psathas,1986a, 1986b, 1990). Sets of directions also appear as *coherent conversational units,* involving organized methods for entering into and for closing the activity. The directions are also

> monitored for their coherence in terms of such matters as the progression of a sequence of operations with orientational and directional references until "arrival" at an end point is proposed. Internally, as the direction set is produced, various matters may be addressed through sequences inserted into the main body of the operations by either party, thereby suspending the sequenced production of operations until a point is reached where both parties agree to resume.

Directions are shown to be collaboratively produced as the recipient is actively involved in listening, showing understandings, giving acknowledgements to the other, and so on. Opportunities are continually provided by the direction giver for the recipient to produce indications of understanding or nonunderstanding, requests for clarification, and so on.

Insight Workshop (from Psathas, 1991, pp. 196-197):
((ring))
1 A: Insight Workshop?
2 C: Yes uh (.) I'm uh (0.4) looking fer Peter Lorenzes class tanite is it meeting at the Academy? (1.0)
3 A: U::h as far as I know it is (0.4) u:m (1.4) thats: the fine print? (0.4) [-or:

```
 4  C:        [ anh the zone system that th[ee
 5  A:              The zone system °oh thats the other one.° um- (1.4)
               yeah that should be meeting eight ta ten thirdy?
 6  C:   Ye:s. (0.2)
 7  A:   Over at (0.4) the Academy. (0.2)
 8  C:   .hh Okay do yu- can you tell me where the Academy is?
 9  A:   Yeah, where ya coming from? (0.2)
10  C:   uh Newton. (0.4)
11  A:   Oka:y why dontcha come up one twenty eight? (0.2)
12  C:   Yes. (0.2)
13  A:   An take two A. (1.))
14  C:   Yes, (.)
15  A:   u:m (0.4) Two A will take ya right across Mass avenoo an ya
         just stay on two A, (0.6) uh until ya get to Lowell Street.
         (1.4)
16  C:   Is it marked? (0.6)
17  A:   uh, Lowell Street? (0.4)
18  C:   Yeah (0.40)
19  A:   a::h Yeah I think there's a street sign there, (.) its a- (0.6) u::m
         (0.6) an inter section with lights.
20  C:   °Okay°
21  A:   an ya turn right on Lowell Street. (1.2) an its about (.) quarter
         to a half a mile (0.4) um, pt (.) take anothyer right on Bartlett
         Avenoo (1.0)
22  C:   °Okay°
23  A:   an that takes ya right to the Academy. (1.0)
24  C:   °Okay° an its one building? (0.2)
25  A:   Yeah, um (0.4) Bartlett avenue sortsuv- sort of curves around
         an (0.2) its a great big school. (0.4)
26  C:   °uh°
27  A:   an they'll be somebody (0.2) near the door taking registrations
         (0.2)
28  C:   °uh°
29  A:   saying=hello=tellin=people=where=to=go. (0.4)
30  C:   °Okay° (0.4) good. (.) tk [ .hh
31  A:                             [okay?
32  C:   Thank=you. (.)
33  A:   yur welcome.=
34  C:   =°bye°=
```

35 A: =bye=
36 C: =bye.

A gross characterization of direction sets such as the one presented in the above transcription can be made prior to a more detailed examination of their sequential structures.

1. They are sequentially organized,
2. they are undertaken in response to a request initiated by the recipient (direction-asker) or solicited by the direction-giver,
3. they are designed for a recipient (direction-asker),
4. they consist of a next turn(s) in which the set of directions is begun,
5. and of next turn(s) in which the recipient-asker co-participates as an active recipient with displays of understanding, acceptance, or requests for elaboration, repetition, clarification, and so on, which are a coordinate part of the set of directions and not new topics,
6. and of a next turn in which the direction-giver proposes "arrival" at the destination,
7. and of a marked ending of the set with such possible moves to end as
   a. an acknowledgment/acceptance/understanding display by the recipient and a move to a next topic or to a closing,
   b. or a request for confirmation by the direction-giver and a confirmation/acknowledgment/appreciation by the recipient and a move to next topic or to a closing.

It is not possible here to go into an elaborate and detailed analysis of these data. A summary of the kinds of findings achieved is listed in part above. Further detailed examination of *openings* or entry into direction-giving shows that there are at least two methods for doing so. *Closings* are revealed to have two parts. *Insertions* within the sequence of directions that are oriented to repair or to requests for clarification, elaboration, and the like, produce a *suspension* of the ongoing main activity. How these suspensions are accomplished is another matter in which close examination of details is required in order to show their patterns and organizations. These various topics are taken up (see Psathas, 1986a, 1986b, 1991) and analyzed.

Thus a particular social action, giving and receiving directions in conversation, is revealed to be an organized phenomenon, one that is socially structured; that is, it involves:

[the] collaborative efforts of both parties in accomplishing its recognizable features. . . . it is occasioned, sequentially organized and responsive to the particulars of the parties (their knowledge, assumed knowledge, displayed understandings, etc.), that is, it is context sensitive. And yet, as a structure, it can be shown to have an organization that is recurrent, orderly and patterned with organized modes of suspension and restorability and with recognizable beginnings and endings, that is, it is context free. [Its structure] is found across any number of direction sets and direction-givers/recipients. (Psathas, 1991, p. 214)

Thus, with regard to the study of sequences in interaction, conversation analysis has discovered the structures of two- and four-part sequences in various types of social actions, and also some structures of sequences extended over a series of turns.

3. SEQUENCE AND STRUCTURE IN INTERACTION

The discovery of structures, of methodical procedures, of the machinery of the production of orderliness in interaction, was an important finding in the development of conversation analysis. A continuing aim of research has been to document discoveries, to focus on particular subsets of recurrent phenomena, and to systematize findings.

Often what appears at first to be a disparate set of observations of some interactional phenomenon can be shown to have an organization, an orderliness. Further, if possible, the systematic properties of that organization could be described and formalized.

In showing how the work on discovering structures proceeded, three examples will be offered: Schegloff's (1979) studies of identification and recognition sequences in telephone conversation openings; Sacks, Schegloff, and Jefferson's (1974) work on the systematic properties of turn-taking in conversation; and Pomerantz's (1978) work on compliments. Each study examined a different phenomenon but worked from within the same methodological perspective.

Identification and Recognition in Telephone Conversation Openings

Telephone conversation openings are different from other types of openings in that the caller knows whom they are calling, although they may not know the person who actually answers. Because the answerer does not know who is calling, they each have a problem of identifying the other, as well as producing some means for each to achieve a possible recognition of the other. Schegloff collected more than 450 calls and examined the first several turns of these opening sequences. He focused on calls in which the answerer's first turn is "Hello" and omitted all service type answers, such as those in which answerer provides the name of a business or service. In these latter types of calls, recognition of the parties is not an issue, and self-identification may be provided in first turn by answerer (e.g., "American Airlines.").

Examples of the calls he considered are the following (numbers of data extracts are from Schegloff's paper):

(42)
    (ring)
1. A: h'llo:?
2. C: hHi:,
3. A: Hi:?

(43)
(ring)
1. A: Hello::
2. C: Hi::::,
3. A: oh: hi:: 'ow are you Agne::s,

After the summons-answer sequence of the telephone ring and the answerer's picking up and speaking, caller's first turn (turn 2) is a greeting that is the first pair part of an adjacency pair. It sets up the conditional relevance for the next speaker's utterance in turn 3 to be a return greeting. But, in addition, it is a claim by speaker that they have recognized the answerer from their voice and have the right to greet them in a less than formal manner. (C: hHi:,). In addition, this greeting also claims that the speaker has the right to be recognized by the answerer from just this voice sample. And indeed, A's return (Hi:?) does indicate a recognition.

One way in which speakers indicate that they do *not* recognize the other party is by withholding the return greeting and thereby producing a short silence that serves as an indication of this. For example:

(45) CF #130
    (ring)
1. A: Hello?
2. C: Hello
        (1.5)

This gap of one and a half seconds indicates that A does not recognize C by their "Hello" and does not immediately produce a return greeting. Instead, what they do produce is the following:

(45) CF #130 continued
3. A: Who's this.

This request for the caller's name indicates that answerer did not have enough resources (i.e., voice sample) to achieve a recognition. Caller may now provide their name or additional talk that might enable answerer to recognize their voice. In this call, the next turn was as follows:

(45) CF #130 continued
4. C: Who is this.= This is your (0.2) friendly goddess,

The caller provides additional voice samples as well as a joking return that could enable the other to recognize them. This serves to identify themselves as someone who should be known to the answerer because their actual name is not used. The other does indeed recognize the caller at this point, as indicated in their next turn (turn 5).

(45) CF #130 continued
5. A: OHhh, hhh, can I ask for a wish

The "OHhh" indicates that success in recognizing the caller has been achieved and the joke is continued.

Thus, in the very first turn by caller (turn 2), an indication that they have recognized the answerer is provided, as well as a claim to be a recognizable person oneself. The failure by the answerer to achieve recognition is indicated by the gap and their ensuing "Who's this." request.

This call also indicates a preference for the achievement of recognition in passing, that is, without calling explicit attention to the matter. If the other can recognize the caller by their first voice sample and greeting ("hello" in turn 2), then their next turn would so indicate and the conversation can continue. But failure to achieve recognition may result in the kinds of troubles and explicit requests for a name as demonstrated in this call.

Another response by answerers is to make it seem that they do recognize the caller, return the greeting, and proceed. This may fail and in next turn they may be "found out," or reveal that they had in fact not recognized the other. For example:

(EN #183)
  (ring)
1. A: Hello
2. B: Hi
3. A: Hi: (.3) oh H̲i̲ Robin

Here, in line 3, A's "Hi:" claims a recognition of B from their "Hi" in turn 2. But three tenths of a second later, A says "oh" and repeats the "Hi," this time with emphasis, and then says the other's name. Prior to the "oh" we can see that A had only *claimed* to have recognized B.

Schegloff goes on to discuss two classes of caller's turns that are specifically directed to identification issues: those concerned with self-identification by caller and those concerned with identification of the answerer. The caller's first turn is not the main place for self-identification to be done. When it is done in this turn it may be of several forms. For example:

a.
(59) (MDE, Supp.)
1. M: hello?=
2. G: =Hello it's me.
3. M: Hi.

A form in which actual name is not used, but recognition is expected by voice or a regularly used type of utterance ("its me").

b.
(64) (LM #199)
1. R: Hello.
2. L: Hi Rob. This is Laurie. How's everything
3. R: ((sniff)) Pretty good. How 'bout you.
4. L: Jus' fine. The reason I called was ta ask ....

(63) (ID #233)
1. I: Hello:,
2. JM: Hello, i- This is Jan's mother.
3. I: Oh yes.
4. JM: Is Jan there by any chance?

In these two instances we see that caller provides a greeting plus a self-identification and moves to a topic immediately. The second example is of the type of opening that can be called the *switchboard request,* where the caller requests to speak to someone other than the answerer. This latter type may occur when the one being asked for is not usually at the place called. In the first example, caller moves to first topic ("How's everything") in this same turn.

More typically, however, it is not caller's first turn where self-identifications are done, but in caller's second turn. What is found routinely in caller's first turn are such utterances as shown in the following instances.

(67) (JG #65)
    1. A: Hello.
→ 2. B: Connie?
    3. A: Yeah Joanie

(71) (RB #185)
    1. A: Hello:?
→ 2. B: Shar'n?
    3. A: Hi!

In the first of these, caller offers a *try-marked* address term, using the other's name with rising intonation, marking the use of the name as a "try." This try may be correct, and the caller's own voice sample may be adequate for the other to recognize them, as occurs in both these cases, the first being strongest in the sense that answerer uses caller's name, though in the second, a greeting term is used and no explicit evidence of recognition is given. Schegloff refers to this as "unevidenced recognition claims." Callers take these claims as displaying recognition and proceed, though it may also happen that they will provide their own name. For example:

(75) (ID #275)
    1. B: 'hhh Hello,
    2. Ba: Hi Bonnie,
    3. B: Hi.=
→ 4. Ba: =it's Barbie.=
    5. B: =Hi

In caller's turn 2 or line 4, they give their name, not presupposing recognition, because answerer did not provide much evidence of having recognized caller.

The try-marked address term also appears to be a *confirmation request*, whereas saying the answerer's name in an assertative or declarative tone, with a terminal intonation, presses the answerer to identify the caller. For example:

(13) (CF #155)
    1. C: Hello?
→ 2. M: Charlie.

The try-marked address term, Schegloff argues, works as a "pre-self-identification sequence." It provides a voice sample; it displays doubt that the recipient will recognize the caller; it provides for a next turn in which the recipient can show if they have achieved recognition; and it allows the caller to project the possibility that they will supply, in their second turn, self-identification by name from which the recipient can achieve recognition. Thus a presequence, or pre-self-identification sequence, provides for a possibility of success without using the less preferred self-identification form and still retains the possibility that explicit self-identification will be provided if this doesn't work out.

Another class of next turns is also equivocal. These are terms such as "yes" or "yeah," which appear to callers as evidence of nonrecognition and they then go on to produce a self-identification. For example:

(78) (JG Supp.)
    1. C: Hello?
    2. S: Hi. Cathy?
→ 3. C: Yeah?
→ 4. S: Stanley.
    5. C: Hi Stan,

By caller's second turn, turn four, recognition is expected without name identification. Sometimes no name is ever given, and it is through the completion of one sequence after another that recognition is shown. Schegloff notes that most frequently when "pre-self-identification" is used in turn 2 , self-identification is produced in turn 4 and a "display of recognition in the next turn so that reciprocal recognition has been achieved" (Schegloff, 1979, p. 57). Nevertheless, even if a name is provided, recognition is not ensured, and similar evidences of trouble (e.g., gap, upgrading of resources) may occur. The variations and instances in which recognition failed are examined by Schegloff to show the significance of recognition in these first turns in conversational openings.

His major finding is that identification is worked out in interactional sequences, turn by turn, and that, rather than an independent structure or organization for identification and recognition, these matters are "overlaid onto sequences of various types" and to particular sequential positions, particularly second turn or caller's first turn. The organization of identification-recognition runs parallel to the other organizations, such as adjacency pair organization, and runs "underground as long as they run compatibly." But if they do not, then identification-recognition takes priority.

The organization that appears to be operating has some "systematically ordered features." These are (Schegloff, 1979, p. 63):

1. Identification of the other by each party is relevant.
2. Identification of the other is relevant at first opportunity.
3. If recognition of/by the other, as one already known, is possible, then it is preferred.
4. Recognitional identification, if relevant and possible, is preferred where identification is relevant.
5. Recognition as an interactional accomplishment has two components: (a) a recognition source and (b) a recognition solution.
6. Preferredly, recognition is "effortless."
7. If the recognition work is done wholly in turns to talk, it may occupy turns addressed to it, or it may inform turns occupied with some other sequential work.
8. If the recognition work is done wholly in turns to talk, the recognition solution should occur in the turn after the recognition source, and should occur contiguously, with no gap.
9. Separation of source and solution exhibits trouble or failure to accomplish the recognition from the resources supplied in the source. Trouble or failure warrant repair.
10. A recognition solution terminates the sequence, unless trouble preceded the solution, in which case a turn component, turn, or sequence of turns diagnostic of the trouble may be added by the speaker of the recognition solution involved.

11. A recognition problem, once solved, is normatively solved for the duration of the conversation.

12. Two types of resources serve as recognition sources: "inspectables" and "self-references." Inspectables include appearance, voice sample, and behavior (e.g., talk) not directed to securing recognition. . . . Self-references include most notably name . . . and self-description.

13. The recognition resources are graded. . . .

14. Recognition from least possible recognition resources sensitive to recipient design is preferred.

15. Should trouble or failure to recognize be displayed, recognizable may offer, or recipient request, supplementary resources. . . .

These findings show that the achievement of identification and recognition in telephone conversation openings is a pervasive issue for the parties and that they utilize systematic procedures for the accomplishment of the task. The methodical character of this work is revealed in Schegloff's analysis, and, although only a few selected examples are presented here, it should be possible for the reader to grasp the way in which the analysis was carried out.

Turn-Taking Organization in Conversation

In the study of turn-taking organization, the major concern of Sacks, Schegloff, and Jefferson (1974) was how to account for the complex system by which parties engaged in talk manage to take turns at speaking. They had noted that speakers speak mainly one at a time, that speaker change occurs quite smoothly, that overlapped speech is brief, and that transitions occur from one turn to the next with very little gap and no overlapped speech. Turn transitions are accomplished in a variety of ways, but there appeared to be some systematic features with regard to how these were done that had not been carefully studied or elaborated by analysts of interaction.

For example (from Sacks, Schegloff, & Jefferson, p. 702):

(a)
    1. Desk: What is your last name [Loraine.
    2. Caller: [Dinnis.
    3. Desk: What?
    4. Caller: Dinnis.

(b)

    1. Jeanette: <u>Oh</u> you know, Mittie- <u>Gor</u>don, eh- <u>Gor</u>don, Mittie's
                     <u>hu</u>sband died
                     (0.3)
    2. Estelle: Oh whe::n.
    3. Jeanette: Well it was in the paper this morning.
    4. Estelle: It <u>wa:</u>:s,
    5. Jeanette: Yeah.

(c)

    1. Fern: Well they're not comin',
    2. Lana: <u>Who</u>.
    3. Fern: Uh Pam, unless they c'n find somebody.

(d)

    1. Guy: <u>Is R</u>ol down by any chance dju know?
    2. Eddy: <u>Huh</u>?
    3. Guy: Is uh Smith down?
    4. Eddy: <u>Y</u>eah <u>he's</u> down,

As these examples show, next speakers' turns occur appropriately, even though a sentence may not be completed and even though the turn may be a single word, phrase, or clause. There is no gap and minimal overlap (except for example (a) where caller, second speaker, speaks their name and overlaps with first speaker's saying their own first name).

In each instance turn transition is accomplished smoothly at turn transition relevance places, and such places are hearably projected. The first speaker stops speaking and the next speaker begins until a completion point, at which point a return to first speaker occurs. Thus speaker change is recurrent.

We can also see that turn length varies and that the size of a turn may be as minimal as one word or a sound (in example (d), turn 2 is "Huh"), which is understandable as a meaningful unit to speakers. Moreover, the topics talked about are variable, as are the social identities of the speakers.

The system of turn-taking they described was one that applied to conversational interaction in general and seemed to be independent of the content or topics talked about, the size of turns, the length of the conversation, and even the number of parties in the conversation. The talk studied could be continuous or discontinuous; that is, the speakers could lapse into silences and resume speaking again, or could be in continuous talk, as in a telephone conversation.

Nevertheless, turn-taking was related to the context and sensitive to whatever was occurring in that context, including the immediately preceding talk. Thus the system of turn-taking was *context sensitive.*

At the same time, it did not seem to matter who the speakers were, the times at which they spoke, the settings in which they spoke, or the topics about which they spoke. In this sense, the system appeared to be *context free*, that is, unaffected by these contextual particulars.

Here of course was a major difference between conventional ethnographic studies and even some of Goffman's analyses of interaction in particular settings, such as total institutions, streets, or public gatherings. The turn-taking system seemed unrelated to the ethnographic particulars of persons, place, and time.

This context free and context sensitive character came to be seen as an important discovery in conversation analysis. It meant that interactional phenomena may not be dependent on the kinds of contextual particulars ordinarily considered to be of utmost importance in the social sciences, for example, such characteristics of persons as age, sex, social class, education, race, religion, and ethnic background; nor such characteristics of social settings as whether the interaction occurred on the street, on the phone, or around the kitchen table. Whether the talk occurred in institutional settings, for example, at school or at work also did not appear to affect the turn-taking system of conversation.

This early formulation of the primacy of the turn-taking system in conversation was in terms of the type of *speech exchange* system to which it seemed to apply. That is, free-flowing conversational interaction in which (a) topics were not predetermined and (b) speaker turns were not preallocated. Alternative speech exchange systems, such as the interview, a debate, a religious ceremony, or a classroom, would have possibly different turn-taking systems because there are restrictions on who may speak, when they may speak, and sometimes in what order they may speak. The study of turn-taking organization in other types of speech exchange systems would require studies that focused on them specifically.

In brief, Sacks et al. (1974) proposed that the turn-taking system for conversation could be described in terms of two components and a set of rules.

TURN-CONSTRUCTIONAL COMPONENT

The type of unit that a speaker may produce could vary, for example, a sentence, a clause, a phrase, or any audible sound. Once under way, the unit projected a completion point, that is, a point at which that type of unit would be completed.

In beginning any unit, the producer was entitled to the amount of time it would take to complete that unit, as having a turn for that unit. When completed, a turn-transition relevance place would be reached, at which point a change of speakers would be possible. Indeed, it was at such points that change of speakers was found to occur.

TURN ALLOCATION COMPONENT

A number of turn-allocation techniques were available to speakers: (a) those that were provided by current speakers selecting the next speaker, and (b) those in which self-selection would be used to begin the next turn.

The system of turn-taking seemed to be organized by a few basic rules.

1.
   a. If the turn-so-far was constructed in such a way that the current speaker selected the next speaker, then the person selected had the right to begin to speak in next turn.
   b. If the turn-so-far was constructed in a way that did not involve "current speaker selects next," then self-selection may be initiated with whoever started first gaining the right to a turn.
   c. If the turn-so-far was constructed in such a way that the current speaker did not select the next, then the current speaker might continue to speak unless someone else self-selected.
2. The system was recursive in that if, at the point when the initial turn unit reached its initial transition relevance place and neither of the rules above (1a or 1b) operated, and if, according to rule 1c the current speaker had continued, then the rules a-c would reapply at the next transition relevance place. This would proceed recursively until a transfer of speakers had occurred.

These rules were ordered such that techniques of turn allocation were themselves ordered; that is, same speaker selects next has priority over next speaker's self-selection.

Furthermore, the "first starter has rights," provided for in rule 1b, orders the possibilities to favor the first speaker over any others and reduces the possibility of many parties self-selecting, which would produce multiple, simultaneous speakers.

Because it is possible for a current speaker to select a next at any time during their speaking, even at the very end of an utterance when they may name a next speaker, the system minimizes the possibility that speakers will self-select until the first relevant transition place is reached. If current speaker continues to speak, thus recycling the rules, self-selection would occur only at the next transition relevance place.

The system thereby minimizes overlap and locates gap (no one's speaking) and overlap possibilities at turn transition-relevance places, rather than just anywhere in the talk.

As a system of rules, the turn-taking systematics were able to account for all of the collected instances of speaker change that Sacks, Schegloff, and Jefferson had amassed over the years. Speaker change occurred at transition-relevance places, the techniques of "current speaker selects next" and self-selection were found to operate at those places, and gap and overlap were minimal.

As a system it was shown to be one that is *self-organizing*, that is, ongoingly done by the parties as they interact; locally produced, in situ, in and of the occasions in which they interact. It is recursive in that it is recycled, orderly, and consistent with all the known instances of turn-taking.

The system can be considered an "ordered optionality system" (Coulter, 1983) because it is not specified what any party *must* do, but rather what options *may* be selected. Conversational interaction may lapse or end. Speakers need not continue to speak. There are no external constraints that operate to produce the systematics.

This analysis of turn-taking in conversation opened up possibilities for the study of varieties of turn-taking systems (i.e., different speech exchange systems) that can be examined, as well as providing a basis for understanding the methodical procedures for accomplishing turn transitions in everyday interaction.

We will proceed with one other example of the discovery of structure in interaction, to indicate the diversity of the earliest studies and the contributions of researchers to the field.

Compliments and Compliment Responses

In her work on compliments, Pomerantz (1978) noted that recipients of a compliment may either agree or disagree with the prior compliment.

But there are many responses that are not either simple acceptances or rejections of the compliment. There appear to be various ways of responding to compliments, including avoiding self-praise, downgrading praise, and shifting the referent of the praise. There are systematic features of these forms of compliment responses, and multiple constraints appear to be operating in the organization of such responses.

One system is that of acceptance or rejection of the compliment where first speaker produces the compliment and next speaker in next turn accepts it.

For example:

KCF:33 (Pomerantz, 1978, p. 84)
    F: That's beautiful it really is
    K: Thank you

In her data, Pomerantz found that appreciations such as "thank you" seemed to be selected over agreements as a way of accepting compliments. In the above example, an agreement without an appreciation would be:

    F: That's beautiful it really is
    K: Yes it is

Acceptances and agreements may occur in combination and/or as alternative responses.

For example:

SBL:2.2.4.-3 (Pomerantz, 1978, p. 85)
    A: Oh it was just beautiful.
    G: Well thank you Uh I thought it was quite nice.....

In this instance, the acceptance in the form of an appreciation ("thank you") and the agreement by G in the form of "nice" follows A's "beautiful."

When a compliment is followed by a rejection, the response may be done with either a disagreement or a qualification of the assertion made in the prior compliment.

For example (hypothetical):

> H: Gee, Hon, you look nice in that dress
> W: Do you really think so? It's just a rag my sister gave me

Here the recipient not only rejects by disagreeing with the "nice," but also offers a second evaluation, which contrasts negatively ("just a rag"). Pomerantz (1978, pp. 87-88) summarizes the relation as follows:

> [W]hile appreciations and agreements are affiliated components . . . they are not sequentially interchangeable. Agreements . . . seem to have more restrictive conditions for their productions. When agreements do co-occur with appreciations, they are preferred routinely after initial appreciations. In short, although appreciations and agreements are interrelated, appreciations over agreements seem to be preferentially selected for accepting compliments. Rejections are routinely performed with disagreements.

However, she went on to try to understand how rejections and disagreements were organized. One system of constraints seemed to govern how recipients would respond to praise. Ordinarily, self-praise is avoided, but when it is done, a speaker may criticize his or her own action, disclaim the self-praise, qualify it, or attribute it to others. When compliments are made that praise the other, there is simultaneously a conflict between the preference for avoiding praise and the preference for accepting and agreeing with compliments. If the compliment is to be agreed with, the recipient would be praising themselves. She found that when presented with praise, recipients produced different forms of responses. One was the praise downgrade, and others were scaled-down agreements with more moderate terms. In such instances, the recipient is agreeing with the praise but not exactly.

For example:

KC4:10 (Pomerantz, 1978, p. 97)
> F: That's beautiful
> K: Is'n it pretty

AP:fn (Pomerantz, 1978: 96)
    B: I've been offered a full scholarship at Berkeley and at UCLA
    G: That's fantastic
    B: Isn't that good
    G: That's marvelous

In both instances, a strong positive term is downgraded to a lesser one
("beautiful" to "pretty" and "fantastic" to "good").

Pomerantz found that when recipients were credited less directly with
referents that could be considered as external to the recipients, that is,
something done by others to or for them, rather than their own actions,
then agreements were more likely to occur. When the praise was more
direct, the recipient was more likely to scale it down.

When disagreements with the prior compliment are made, they may
also be done by proposing that the giver has overdone, exaggerated, or
been excessive.

NB:5 (Pomerantz, 1978, p. 98)
    A: ...you've lost suh much weight
    P: Uhh hmhh uhh hmhh well, not _that_ much

AP:FN (Pomerantz, 1978, p. 99)
    A: Good shot
    B: Not very solid though

Following such disagreement, those who offered the praise may chal-
lenge or not agree with the qualifications or moderations of the recipient
and reassert the praise in next turn.

For example:

AP:FN (Pomerantz, 1978, p. 99)
    A: Good shot
    B: Not very solid though
    A: Ya' get any more solid, you'll be terrific

Two other types of response to a compliment are to shift the referent
of the compliment or to return the compliment.

WS:YMC. -4 (Pomerantz, 1978, p. 102)
    R: You're a good rower, Honey.
    J: These are very easy to row. Very light

Here the recipient shifts from himself to the type of boat and attributes the praise as relevant for the boat rather than himself. Credit may thus be shifted away from the self and even to others.

MC (Pomerantz, 1978, p. 105)
    C: Ya' sound (justiz) real nice
    D: Yeah you soun' real good too

Such return compliments may work to end the praise sequence.

In her examination of these varieties of responses to compliments, Pomerantz was able to show that there were systematic features. There appeared to be two systems operating. One is of responses that "legitimize, ratify, affirm, etc., prior compliments." A second system is one of avoiding praise. This may be done by downgrading the praise or shifting the referent of the praise to other-than-self, with another form represented by returning the compliment.

Thus Pomerantz could show by a careful examination of a large number of collected compliments and their responses that there were not only certain empirical tendencies, but more significantly, that there were systematic features for the ways in which such responses were organized. Sequences of interaction with regard to this type of social action were found not to be random, but rather systematically organized.

Pomerantz's work on compliments illustrated how the collection of instances of ordinary interaction from a variety of data sources could illuminate a particular interactional phenomenon and show its systematic properties.

In contrast, Goffman's (1971) illustrations of such matters as *remedial interchanges, supportive interchanges, access rituals*, and so on are presented within a theory of conformity and deviation from social norms, how such "moves" function in interaction, and how the individual is related to the social structures in which they may find themselves. Individuals' utterances are treated as moves that have significance in a series of actions between "offenders" and the "offended" when deviations from norms occur. Thus remedial interchanges are examined in terms of their function in, for example, restoring the social order by correcting failures to live up to expectations. Similarly, supportive interchanges represent moves that have a ritual character in achieving restoration, reducing damage, producing apologies or excuses, or minimizing blame.

For example, with regard to remedial interchanges, he offers the following example: "One pedestrian trips over another, says 'Sorry,' as he passes, is answered with 'okay,' and each goes on his way.

" . . . three different elements are involved. . . . First . . . the offense, offender and victim. Second, is the ritual work that is performed in the situation. Here the apology and its acceptance. Third, is the 'deed' the act . . . which otherwise might be an offense but for the ritual that is performed in association with it, this work functioning to modify the worst possible implications of what in fact has occurred" (Goffman, 1971, p. 139).

His presentation is in a section introduced by saying that he will be considering "moral rules and their function as the link between self and society" (p. 138). This led to a consideration of deviation from the rules and the ritual dialogue that provides a remedy. Remedial activities can be found in interchanges occurring at the everyday level. Among adults, he says, "almost every kind of transaction including every coming together into a moment of talk, is opened and closed by ritual, if not remedial then supportive" (Goffman would interpret greeting exchanges analyzed by conversation analysis as instances of supportive interchanges or access rituals). "This infuses into every area of life . . . a constant checking back to, and reminder of, a small number of central beliefs about the rights and character of persons."

This cited instance represents, for Goffman, an exemplification of remedial work, of how deviations are remedied and, presumably, social order restored. They illustrate the way in which the moral order can be found at the level of the everyday.

Goffman's approach here is seen to be distinctively different from conversation analysis. He starts with a theory of moral order and locates everyday examples of remedies for transgressions. He formulates these interchanges as rituals: "perfunctory, conventionalized act(s) through which an individual portrays his respect and regard for some object of ultimate value or to its stand in" (Goffman, 1971, p. 62), and interprets their significance for the reestablishment of the moral order. That is, he uses ritual as a preformed classification system designed to collect a range and variety of empirical (and hypothetical) examples. His elaboration of their variations and his examination of their occurrence in different settings is designed to show their range, distribution, and frequency. This offers support for his claims about their social significance and for his theoretical interpretations, which postulate their ubiquity and generality. Thus instances are selected by Goffman as exemplifications of his theoretical formulations concerning normative order, and not as interactional phenomena whose formal structures or machinery or methodical procedures are to be described and analyzed as phenomena in their own right.

Whereas conversation analysts try to maintain close attention to the systematic features of the production of social actions (e.g., taking turns, exchanging greetings, giving and receiving compliments), Goffman interprets such actions as instantiations of his theorizing about normative order. Nevertheless, Goffman's attention to actions at the level of the everyday, and his emphasis on their importance, provided additional support for the work of conversation analysts.

We have seen thus far how conversation analysis focused on the discovery, description, and analysis of sequential structures of interaction and how these studies differ from other approaches. Next we will describe the methodological approach and perspective of conversation analysis in order to specify its distinctive character.

4. THE METHODOLOGICAL PERSPECTIVE OF CONVERSATION ANALYSIS

The methodological perspective adopted by conversation analysts may be characterized as an analytic approach that seeks to describe and analyze social actions, the organizational features of various, naturally occurring, interactional phenomena. The basic orientation is one of discovering and analyzing such phenomena.

Order is assumed. The problem is to discover, describe, and analyze that order or orderliness.

There is, in general, no interest in the ethnographic particulars of persons, places, and settings. Rather, the interest is in discovering structures of interaction, the orderliness of phenomena that are independent of cohort particulars (Garfinkel & Sacks, 1970); that is, the orderliness does not depend on particular persons or particular settings.

The variety of interactional phenomena available for study are not selected on the basis of some preformulated theorizing, which may specify matters of greater or lesser significance. Rather the first stages of research have been characterized as *unmotivated looking*. Data may be obtained from any available source, the only requirement being that these should be naturally occurring, rather than produced for the purpose of study, as in the case of laboratory experiments or controlled observations. In practice, this has meant interactional phenomena that would have occurred regardless of whether the researcher had come upon the scene; therefore, conversations, news interviews, therapy sessions, telephone calls, dinner table talk, police calls, as well as all manner of interactional phenomena that the researcher may be able to come upon and record are potential data sources.

Recordings, whether audio or video, are essential. In some settings, or when research is supported by grants, permissions may be obtained in writing from all those participating. Protection of rights to privacy are assured, and individual participants may be anonymized and not identified.

Generally speaking, the mundane nature of most of the kinds of interactional phenomena studied raise hardly any issue concerning privacy. In addition, the fact that researchers are concerned with interaction in its own right, rather than with the particular persons or places or institutions providing the data, serves to alleviate concerns about privacy. The types of interactions studied are so common and so recurrent

45

that refusals are not a problem because, generally speaking, there are numerous various alternative sources available.

The key issue in obtaining recordings is that the interaction can be repeatedly replayed and transcribed. Although transcription is a necessary step in the process of analysis, the retention of original recordings makes possible repeated re-viewings and re-listenings. In the process of such repetitions, many previously unnoticed aspects of the interaction may be noticed and focused upon.

Another set of reasons for the requirement of recordings is that because no preselection of topics or phenomena is generally made by the researcher, it is not possible to simply seek out a particular phenomenon. Rather, a wider net is cast, and many matters remain unstudied but available for later reexamination and discovery. In addition, the phenomena are seemingly simple but complex, with temporal sequences of sometimes split-second timing, so that they are not capturable by ordinary observation, which relies on the senses and memory. But it is not the deficiency of observational systems and the use of the senses that are the only issues. Rather, it is that recordings provide the opportunity for repeated viewings and listenings, and the very process of transcription often reveals interactional phenomena that had been hitherto unnoticed.

Thus the phenomena that are discovered are the result of a process of repeated listening/viewings and transcribings. Numerous instances of similar phenomena, or singular instances of structurally complex and transparently significant phenomena, may be collected. When collections of numerous instances are made, the possibility for the study of varieties and variations is also made possible.

In more recent work, when there is a focus on interaction within particular institutional or organizational settings, then the collection may be of numerous and varied types of interaction in the settings, for example, calls to the police and the subsequent handling of them, radio transmissions between computer-operating airport dispatchers, news interviews, and so on.

The interactional phenomena include utterances and activities, embodied actions and movements, as well as "talk." A major requirement is that the matters selected for study are those that persons in the setting are themselves demonstrably aware of and/or oriented to in the course of their actions. This rules out such matters as micro measurements of, for example, physical distances or the rapidity of talk, except as these are observably noticed and oriented to by the participants themselves during the ongoing course of the interaction itself, or in subsequent activities, for example, talking about something that happened earlier.

No assumptions are made regarding the participants' motivations, intentions, or purposes; nor about their ideas, thoughts, or understandings; nor their moods, emotions, or feelings; except insofar as these can demonstrably be shown to be matters that participants themselves are noticing, attending to, or orienting to in the course of their interaction. Further, if and when this happens, their doing so is done "for all practical purposes, in and of that situated and occasioned production. What is available to the hearer for such 'apprehendings' is similarly available to the observer" (Psathas, 1990, p. 7).

There are restrictions introduced into the conversation analyst's use of participants' past relationships, biographies, and interests; as well as about their past beliefs, thoughts, or hopes, and so on. The researcher's analysis of what they are now doing is not to be based on some constructive analytic interpretation of such matters as "taking the role of the other," "presenting a self," "managing impressions," "being deviant," "defining the situation," and the like. All such constructive analytic interpretations are set aside, because they interfere with the direct examination of the phenomena themselves. Thus conversation analysts are not trying to explain phenomena drawing on some theoretical, explanatory framework, but are trying to describe and analyze them.

Also, no attempt is made to generalize to similar instances or ones that the researcher claims to know from past experience or knowledge. Recalled or imagined instances are not admissable as proof or support or corroboration of claims about the actual phenomenon. Rather, only repeated instances of other *demonstrably* similar empirical instances are admissible, provided these are also available in recorded form. Otherwise it would be the researcher's word that there are additional exactly similar instances, a word offered without proof.

It is a further constraint on conversation analysis that the reports written must include the transcripts of the data that represent the phenomena analyzed. This inclusion of the original data in the written or presented report is an important methodological constraint that is not met by most other forms of research on interaction. The constraint is more rigorous, however, in that it is expected that even the original recordings can and would be made available to others to examine directly and review.

This is in contrast to field research reports of interaction and to descriptive or analytic reports based on codings of interaction. Such studies cannot make available the original occurrences of the phenomena reportedly collected, observed, and analyzed, to enable others to examine the actual particulars, the ordering, movement, and audio, spatial, temporal organization of the phenomena themselves. In such studies the interactional phenomena have been modified and transformed into *reported interactions,* and we are left only with the possibility of discussing the reports, rather than examining the data on which the reports are based.

It may be helpful to consider here what conversation analysts have meant by interactional phenomena. They have such characteristics as the following:

1. A visual and/or auditory and/or tactual and/or kinesthetic appearance for the participants in the actual course of their interaction
2. A spatio-temporal appearance, which includes speech, utterances, silences, and bodily movements; synchronous actions within and between individual persons; and relationships between such synchronous actions; in and as these are situated productions

In simpler terms, interactional phenomena are talk and action in a situation that may include oriented-to features of the setting as well as other persons.

The examination of *inter*actional phenomena refers to how they are patterned, arranged, and audio-spatio-temporally organized in the course of their production by a participant; how they are organized *between* the participants; and/or both of the above.

Analysts are oriented to the discovery, identification, description, and analysis of such matters as the audio-spatio-temporal course of interactional phenomena; their constituent elements; their pattern, synchrony, and coordination; their sequential properties; and the *betweenness* of their production, that is, the ways in which other parties are interrelated in the ongoing course of interaction.

Descriptions and analyses try to note, in detail, how a phenomenon appears in the course of its *actual* production. Questions as to the meanings of actions are answered by direct examination of "what happened before" and "what follows next," taking into account the manner in which participants themselves display that they make sense (meaning) of what occurs.

Because conversation analysis seeks to remain faithful to members' perspectives, it is important not to use knowledge based on what happens subsequently to interpret what preceded. For the participants, only that which immediately preceded is available to them as they ongoingly produce their actions. They cannot know what their actions *will* come to because the future has not yet happened. The researcher, because the tape is available, may be tempted to look ahead and draw on the actual outcomes of actions, and attribute to the prior actions an intended or anticipated outcome similar to what actually occurred. If the member's perspective is to be taken seriously, however, the researcher must be careful to restrict himself or herself to only those matters that are also available to members, namely, what has just been said and done, and not what is later arrived at.

This methodological constraint is difficult to maintain and often results in what appears to be an analysis that does not utilize all the available information. After all, it is possible to see or hear on the tape what finally happened. Therefore it is easy to attribute to the participants such matters as intentions and plans to have things come out exactly that way. But such interpretations use information that is unavailable to participants *as* they interact. Such knowledge of what an interaction came to (i.e., the future) has to be set aside and not used to make sense or to explain what it was that participants were doing. This is not to deny that actions project nexts, that is, are sequentially implicative, as we saw in the case of a first pair part of an adjacency pair. Nor is it to deny that persons may orient their actions to what may come next, to anticipations and expectations. But, if this is so, then it must be demonstrable in their actions, in what they actually say and do, and not assumed by the analyst. That members consider, talk about, and explicitly orient to next actions is clear. That utterances provide for possible inferences with regard to future courses of action is also clear. How they do this, in just what ways and by what means they do so, are matters to be studied and demonstrated by the examination of concrete instances.

Because the researcher's focus is restricted to the description and analysis of a particular interactional phenomenon, further study may be oriented to a search for additional instances of the same phenomenon, so that its variations may be described. Other, seemingly similar but nevertheless different phenomena may be uncovered in this process.

Such matters as the social distribution of the phenomenon, for example, its presence among different cultural groupings, races, classes, or categories of persons or types of situations, are not, generally speaking, matters of concern or attention for conversation analysts. Their primary task, difficult enough, is the discovery, description, and analysis of complex interactional phenomena as socially produced phenomena in their own right. Such questions as their frequency, range, and distribution may be pursued in other inquiries, but they are not relevant in terms of providing proof or validation of a claim about the structure of an interactional phenomenon.

Here we must say something about what has been called the *method of instances*, which constitutes the methodological and epistemological position of conversation analysis. (See also an excellent discussion of this matter by Benson & Hughes, 1991, pp. 130-132.)

An instance of something is an occurrence. One instance is sufficient to attract attention and analytic interest. The instance is, after all, an event whose features and structure can be examined to discover how it is organized. Whether it does or does not occur again is irrelevant for the task of showing how this single occurrence is organized, what the machinery of its production is. That this particular social action occurred is evidence that the machinery for its production is culturally available, involves members' competencies, and is therefore possibly (and probably) reproducible. Its recurrence, however, is not proof of the adequacy of an analysis, because the analytic task is to provide a wholly adequate analysis of just how *this* instance is organized. Additional instances provide "another example of the method in the action, rather than securing the warrantability of the description of the machinery itself" (Benson & Hughes, 1991, p. 131).

This is also not a question of sampling from a population of occurrences because, in advance of an analysis, it is not possible to say what a particular instance is a sample of. Collections of instances cannot be assembled in advance of an analysis of at least one, because it cannot be known in advance what features delineate each case as a "next one like the last."

Formal descriptions of social actions capture and display the features of the machinery that was sufficient to produce the interactional phenomenon, in *this* case, in *its details*, in just the way it occurred. This is not therefore an abstract generalization that glosses the particulars of an instance. It should be clear that conversation analysis is not achieving "empirical generalizations," but rather is concerned with providing analyses that meet the criteria of "unique adequacy" (Garfinkel & Sacks, 1970).

The mechanisms that produce a phenomenon may be a set of a priori methods that members use (Coulter, 1983). In this respect, these methods would be found in each and every instance of the production of that particular phenomenon. The analysis of the "machinery of turn-taking" in conversation shows that this machinery organizes the sequential order of turns at talk, recurrently and over many instances. But its structure, as a mechanism, is not based on empirical frequencies. By analogy, it may be compared to the "rules of chess," where the rules are not based on the frequency with which persons engage particular rules in their play. Rather, each game, if it is chess, is organized by a set of rules that allow the game to be chess rather than some other game. This is the machinery for the production of actions that are "playing the game of chess" and, presumably, that structure could be discerned by examining one instance of the play of the game.

This analogy is offered as an aid to the reader, but it is not meant to imply that the machinery or the methodical procedures for the production of some interactional phenomenon are to be considered as a set of rules. There are various kinds of mechanisms and methodical procedures. Their features and structures cannot be prespecified. Each must be studied to provide an analysis that is *uniquely adequate* for that particular phenomenon.

"Questions of meaning are generally answered by strict reference to the actual course of interaction by observing what happens first, second, next, etc., by noticing what preceded it; and by examining what is actually done and said by the participants" (Psathas, 1990, p. 13). First efforts to characterize actions may rely on the researcher's own competencies as a member of the culture, sharing the same language. Understandings of what is occurring may draw on such general competencies. However, claims made about meanings must be modified to conform to the actual occurrences because, in their interactions, persons may produce actions that are not congruent with the researcher's first interpretations of what was happening. For example, what appears to the observer to be a "question" may not be followed by an "answer." If a prior utterance is not responded to as a question, its meaning for the parties is to be found in what they actually do next. The question may not have been heard, or may have been misunderstood or evaded. An answer may have been delayed. Or the question may be responded to as an invitation in the form of a question. As an invitation, the next turn may display an acceptance or declination. Or the utterance may be heard as a compliment (e.g., "aren't you looking great tonight") and responded to with a return compliment (e.g., "so are you"). Thus preliminary characterizations of an utterance-type or turn-type may be modifiable as an analysis proceeds. The key issue is to examine how members themselves make sense of what is said. Thus meanings are seen to be contingent, locally accomplished, situated, and conventional.

Once a particular interactional phenomenon is discovered, identified, and analyzed, it may be relevant to examine additional materials, that is, already collected, recorded, and/or transcribed interactions, to find further instances and to accumulate a collection. Collections may result in rich discoveries, which reveal that the original phenomenon is more complex than first noted; or that a second instance is found to be not an instance like the first, but rather a different phenomenon in itself.

Schegloff (1979, 1986), in his studies of telephone conversation openings, has done this over many years and, with a corpus of more than 500 openings, has been able to focus on such matters as summons-answer sequences, greeting exchanges, identification and recognition sequences, and so on. The same has been done with repairs (Schegloff, Jefferson, & Sacks 1977); closings (Button, 1987, 1990; Schegloff & Sacks, 1973); compliments and responses (Pomerantz, 1978); lists (Jefferson, 1990); invitations, offers, and rejections (Davidson, 1990); and direction-giving (Psathas, 1986a, 1986b, 1991).

Such collections can then be examined carefully to discover archetypical patterns and variations (cf. Schegloff on openings, 1979, 1986; Button on closings, 1990). The variations can be examined to analyze and describe their features, to develop characterizations of types of variations, to discover sequence types, for example, patterns characteristic of types of utterances in sequential utterances. Such patterns may be of two or four or multiple parts.

Or, if the phenomenon originally studied is located in the initial part of a two-part sequence involving speaker change, the varieties of responses by second speaker to the varieties of initial utterance types may be examined. Examples are Button's (1990) examination of varieties of closings and Davidson's (1990) study of modifications of invitations, offers, and rejections.

Button further shows how movements out of closings can produce a variety of closing types and how speakers can negotiate for conversation termination or continuation. His work extends earlier work by

Schegloff and Sacks on the opening up of closings (Schegloff & Sacks, 1973).

Studies have become cumulative and have

expanded and deepened our understanding of interactional phenomena. What may have begun as a first noticing, a discovery of a particular interactional phenomenon, with a detailed description and analysis of a single instance, continues, with a collection of instances, to reveal rich complexit(ies) and diversit(ies) of the phenomenon, the varieties of its forms, and the interactional "work" that it accomplishes within particular contexts." (Psathas, 1990, p. 17)

Because researchers must make available, in transcripts and published extracts, the data on which their studies are based, other researchers may then examine the same, as well as additional, materials, and either replicate or extend the analyses first presented. The aim of a social science of replicable and cumulative findings with regard to important social phenomena can thus be, and has already been, realized.

This science, in Sacks's (in Atkinson & Heritage, 1984, p. 21) words, "describes methods persons use in doing social life . . . [and shows] the detailed ways in which actual, naturally occurring social activities occur and are subjectable to formal description."

5. TALK AND SOCIAL STRUCTURE

Another direction in which research studies have moved has been to examine the structures of interaction in institutional and work settings.

These studies are referred to by some as studies of *talk and social structure* or *institutional talk*. Such studies consider that some of the interactional phenomena observed may, to some extent, be related to the particular settings in which they occur, or that the focus of the research should be to better understand how work settings are organized.

Since its inception, conversation analysis has examined interaction in a variety of work or organizational settings, beginning with Sacks's own inquiries at the Suicide Prevention Center. Subsequent studies have examined interaction in courtrooms (Atkinson & Drew, 1979; Maynard, 1984; Pollner, 1979), doctors' offices (Frankel, 1984, 1989, 1990; Heath, 1984; Ten Have, 1991), and among the police (Meehan, 1989; Whalen, 1994; Zimmerman, 1992), as well as news interviews (Heritage & Greatbatch, 1991), broadcast news (Clayman, 1988), political speeches (Atkinson, 1984), and various media events.

The issue researchers face in such studies is how to relate the interactional phenomena studied to the so-called larger context of the organization or institutional setting in which they occur. One problem is how to conceptualize social structure in ways that do not simply borrow earlier sociological formulations of the nature and character of social structure as though it is some sort of ontological entity. That is, the problem is how *not* to reify social structure. In conventional sociological approaches, social structure is often formulated as having, if not a determining effect on all interaction, at least an influence or shaping effect. All interaction is thus considered to be affected, and therefore to some extent explained, by the context in which it occurs. When that context is defined as macro-social structural in nature, the tendency of some analysts is to *assume* that such effects operate pervasively, rather than trying to show in exactly what ways the activities of persons in the settings are constrained, organized, or shaped. Conversation analysis would propose to show in what ways persons orient to, take into account, and make relevant particular features of the setting; in what ways the settings' features provide enabling conditions for particular kinds of activities; in what ways the parties are engaged in what constitutes the work of the organization, and thereby are engaged in producing interaction that is context renewing and re-forming. That is, in what ways are the parties reproducing the very structure that is commonsensically believed to be external and constraining?

As an example, consider the company that is providing a package pickup and delivery service (Psathas, 1992). The work of the company includes answering the telephone, taking orders from customers, determining what it is that is to be picked up, where it is located, where it is to be delivered, who will pay for the service, and so on. Is a telephone call and the interaction between the employee and the caller requesting a service to be considered *only* as a telephone call, and to be analyzed in terms of openings, closings, turn-taking, and so on? Indeed not. In the call, the parties are engaged in carrying out the services of the company; callers present themselves as customers for those services; and the completed call incorporates various aspects of the information needed for the company to carry out its services.

For example:
(Call to a package pickup and delivery service; A is answerer and C is caller)

Call # 1
1. A: thanks=for=calling Choice, Melanie speaking.
2. C: hi Melanie I'm calling from Bernard Morse Hospital Cytology
3.   Lab?// ( )
4. A: //okay you'd like a pick=up? (1.5)
5. C: pardon (.2) ye//ah
6. A: //you'd like (.) a package (.) picked up?
7. C: yeah//we need something picked up.=
8. A: //uh
9. A: =uh- kay (.) what hospital is that again?
10. C: uh- its Be:r:nard Mo:rse Ho:spital in Na::tick, ((spoken slower, stretched and more pronounced))
11. A: okay hold o//n

Call # 8
1. A: thanks for calling Choice, Melanie speaking.
2. C: hi this is Nan from the World Trade Center
3. A: okay you'd like a pickup?
4. C: yes
5. A: can I have your account number?

Call #9
1. A: thanks for calling Choice, Melanie speaking.
2. C: hello this is Mary Weber I'm calling from Mutual Capital

Call #7
1. A: thanks for calling Choice, Melanie speaking.
2. C: hi Loreen?
3. A: Melanie
4. C: oh Melanie, I'm sorry.
5. A: that's okay can I help you?
6. C: yeah this is Paul from the Woburn office. I gotta job here.
7. A: okay do you have the account number?

Several activities that are work activities are carried out in the course of the call by the parties. This work is done interactionally and collaboratively. In what can be seen as turn-by-turn interactions, which have all the characteristics of adjacency pair structures, self-identifications, recognitions, questions and answers, requests, and so on, are also found the ongoing work of taking orders, getting billing information, determining who is calling, from where and to where a package is to be picked up and delivered, and so on. Clearly, an analysis restricted to the study of such interactional structures as adjacency pairs would not enable us to understand the ways in which the various tasks of the parties are being done. An issue faced by researchers then is how to combine these two analytic concerns, how to incorporate and study that which had been "suspended" or specifically disattended, namely, the institutional or work setting in which the participants are actively engaged in "doing the work of the organization," as well as the way in which they constitute and reproduce through their activities the social structures of action and relationships.

As Boden and Zimmerman (1991, p. 12) formulate this issue, if the mechanisms of "mundane conversation organize the basic forms of social action and interaction out of which patterns of repetitive activity taken to be evidence of social structure are built," then talk-in-interaction contributes to the "constitution of institutional settings (and the production of social structure)." Studies will then show how talk-in-interaction "enables institutional modes of conduct." Such studies would show us how talk-in-interaction is "selected, adapted and combined or configured to reflexively produce and reproduce social structure." From this view, talk-in-interaction represents an avenue to understanding how social structures are produced.

In the calls excerpted above, the opening sequences can be analyzed to show how answerer provides, in first turns, self-identification both by first name and name of her company, indicates her availability to provide service, and offers appreciation for the call to this particular company. The character of a service organization is immediately furnished for the caller. If speed of making requests for service and obtaining the service are an issue, this first opening turn solves several problems for the caller. It indicates that they have reached *this* company, that the answerer is prepared to *represent* the company, that her name *differentiates* her from other answerers or service providers and makes her *accountable* for follow-up calls or complaints. This first turn enables caller to obtain a sense of how this company and service are organized, namely, that the telephone answerer may be the only person they need to speak with in order to obtain the service they need, or that the telephone answerer may be able to switch them to any other more relevant person if they are unable to answer a particular request, because they answer for the company.

In this way, and with attention to this level of detail, it is possible to show how the work of the company is being accomplished and how the parties are ongoingly producing its character and organization.

In contrast to conversation analysis, analytic summaries of such calls might be stated in general terms, such as "the company provides a service operator to answer every call and determine what service the caller needs." Or, in the language of role theory, "the role of the service operator is to determine what each caller needs, obtain such information as name and location of caller, whether they have an account with this company, what is to be picked up, where, and to whom and where it is to be delivered, and the like." Such formulations gloss the details and the organization of activity at the work site, formulate it in general terms, present an idealized version of the activities, and propose that this pattern represents the structure or the institutional character of activities. Viewed retrospectively and through the lens provided by theoretically derived concepts, the activities achieve the character of determinate courses of action, socially structured patterns, virtually existent, or "thinglike" in their character. This "retrospective illusion" (Merleau-Ponty, 1968) provides for the characterization of such structures as "determining" or "causing" or "affecting" human actions in the setting, thereby losing their ongoing, contingent, and interactional character.

Human actions may *constitute* social structures and institutions, but the ordinariness, repetitiveness, and locally achieved detail of their organization, involving the collaboratively produced activities by members of society, is somehow lost in such accounts. Conversation analysis or talk-in-interaction, as an ethnomethodological approach and perspective, is concerned with retaining their character and focusing on the details of their production.

It has been ethnomethodology's

> fundamental insight . . . that the primordial site of social order is found in members' use of methodical practices to produce, make sense of, and thereby render accountable, features of their local circumstances. . . . The socially structured character of . . . any enterprise undertaken by members is thus not exterior or extrinsic to their everyday workings, but interior and intrinsic, residing in the local and particular detail of practical actions undertaken by members uniquely competent to do so. (Boden & Zimmerman, 1991, pp. 6-7)

The respecification of the problem of social order by ethnomethodology therefore treats the "problem of social order" as completely internal to the sites studied. It conceives "social settings as self organizing and for just that reason has no further need for the received concepts of 'social actor' and 'social structure' " (Sharrock & Button, 1991, p. 141).

Calls to Emergency

As an example of the type of analysis that is possible, we shall consider studies of calls to the police, a form of call that may more broadly be characterized as a "service call" (Zimmerman, 1992).

Here are two calls to 9-1-1, an emergency or police service in most American cities.

(1.)
```
    [17]{MCE/21-25/35}
01  D:    Mid-City Emergency
02  C:    can I've thuh police=please=
03  D:                            =thisis police.
04  C:    O:h uh there's .hh suh lou' music over on .........
```

(2.)
    [18] [MCE/21-20/27]
01   D: Mid-City Emergency
02   C: .hh Hi we gotuh:
03   This iz security atthuh bus
04   depot=Greyhound bus depot?=
05   D: =Umhm
06   C: An we gotuh guy down here that's uh: over intoxicated ....

As calls to the police, these calls illustrate that opening sequences may deal with issues of recognition and identification, but in a different fashion from calls between acquaintances.

Zimmerman (1992), referring to these kinds of openings, points out that the answerer's first turn is designed for anonymous callers who have a primary interest in learning whether they have reached the intended place. Callers expect to contact someone who can act as an agent of that organization. The answerer's self-identification confirms this, whether the first turn is "Mid-City police" or "county dispatch" or "9-1-1 emergency." They can immediately align themselves in their particular situated identities as *complaint taker* and *dispatcher* for the answerer, and *complainant* or *seeker of service* for the caller. At various times in the call, the particular identities, that is, "who is who when," are a matter of what the interaction is about. That is, dispatcher may become interrogator and caller may become interogatee. Their situated identities can be shown to be oriented to by the other party in the interaction.

The opening that provides name of place called facilitates a move to first topic or reason for call. As shown in the second call, caller can move to first topic in caller's first turn once the answerer has self-identified as "Mid-City Emergency." There are no greeting exchanges, how-are-yous, or named self-identifications by caller. Such matters are routinely produced in *noninstitutional calls*, such as calls to acquaintances. In a call to emergency, such matters are shown by the parties to not be relevant. The nature of the emergency and its description appear to be the important business of the call.

In the first call, we see that caller's first turn did address issues of identification because caller requests "police=please." It is possible that the dispatcher's first turn self-identification as "Mid-City Emergency" was not recognized or understood as equivalent to "police." However, once the identification is made in dispatcher's next turn, "This is police," the caller moves immediately to the topic or reason for the call.

Both calls illustrate, therefore, that once self-identification is recognized and understood by callers to the police emergency number, they can and do move to the topic or reason for the call. That the call is impersonal and instrumental is exhibited by the nonrelevance of recognition of the caller by the answerer. The immediate move to the reason for the call (and the acceptance of this move by the answerer) shows that both parties are oriented to the type of activity they are engaged in, namely, asking for and providing assistance.

The way in which a focus on the urgency of the need is achieved is exhibited for the participants themselves in the sequences of their actions. At the same time, they are also constituting the locally achieved "institutional context" of the call.

For the purpose of the call, relevant identities are being produced and displayed by the parties. Answerer (dispatcher) self-identifies with the name of the place and the type of service it offers ("Mid-City Emergency"), and callers' presentations of reasons for the call display that they are persons who are involved or concerned about matters for which the police are being summoned. In the second call, the caller self-identifies as "security atthuh bus depot" as well as describing the kind of conduct and location for which help is being sought. In the first call, without any self-identification, caller locates himself in proximity to the "lou' music" and is about to describe its location, thereby displaying a relevant identity as the complainant.

Thus, as Zimmerman concludes (1992, p. 49), "the openings of calls for help . . . put in play relevant identities and initiate (as well as withhold) sequences of interaction that enable participants to manage the interactional issues involved in contact between anonymous parties seeking and providing help."

In studies such as this, the researcher is examining interactional structures but is oriented to discovering and describing how these structures are relevant for as well as constitutive of the organization, institution, or work setting in which they occur. There is no claim to any particular type of opening being universal; but rather, the analysis shows how the call is organized and how it accomplishes the work of the organization. As Zimmerman demonstrates in this study, it is also possible to compare the type of interaction occurring here with the structures of interaction found in mundane conversation. Such comparisons enable a characterization of the situation being studied as having "distinctive features" that differ from mundane conversation.

Perspective Display Sequences

A study by Maynard (1991) focused on several clinics that specialized in such developmental disabilities as autism and mental retardation. Children were extensively evaluated, and then clinicians met with the child's parents to inform them of the findings and diagnoses as well as to present recommendations for dealing with specific problems. These sessions or informing interviews might last anywhere from 20 minutes to 2 hours. At the beginning of these sessions, the clinicians often formulate the purpose of the interview as being the report of findings and of recommendations. When clinicians ask patients for their view or perspective, they may do so before delivering their findings. In this way some matters elicited from the parents can then be used by the clinicians in the formulation of their report. They can learn what and how much parents know concerning the child and they can formulate agreement or degrees of agreement with the parents' perspective.

Thus Maynard formulates the generic form of a perspective display series (PDS) as consisting of three turns:

1. clinician's opinion query or perspective display invitation
2. recipient's reply or assessment
3. clinician's report and assessment

The first two turns can be considered a "presequence," in that they provide for an entry into the delivery of the news, but are not in themselves the places where the news is presented. Depending on what happens in the presequence, alternative trajectories in next turns are possible. For example, the asker may follow a reply with his own report. At other times, "the reply to a perspective display invitation will be followed by further questions or other topicalizers that permit the recipient to talk at length on some topic" (p. 168). Nevertheless, in these sequences, the diagnosis is eventually delivered.

Clinicians were found to "fit their diagnostic news delivery to the occasioned display of the parents' perspective, especially by formulating agreement in such a way as to 'co-implicate' the parents' perspective in the diagnostic presentation." The analysis of how this is done is fairly lengthy and cannot be presented here. Instead, we will describe some of Maynard's findings concerning different perspective display invitations and their consequences.

Maynard found that there are two major types of invitations to parents to present their perspective, that is, how they view the child. One is a *marked* and the other an *unmarked* invitation. A marked invitation refers to the problem as somehow being "possessed" by the child.

(1.)

    (8.013)

    Dr. E: What do you see? as- as his difficulty.

                (1.2)

    Mrs. C: Mainly his uhm: (1.2) the fact that he doesn't understand everythin. (6) and also the fact that his speech. (.7) is very hard to understand what he's saying.

(2.)

    (14.012 Simplified)

    Dr. E: What do you think is his problem

                (3.)

    Dr. E: I think you know him better than all of us really. So that ya know this really has to be a (.8) in some ways a (.6) team effort to (4) understand what's (.4) going o:::n. .hh

    Mrs. D: Well I know he has a- (.6) a learning problem (1.2) in general. .hhh and s::::peech problem an' a language problem. (1.) a behavior problem, I know he has all o' that but still .hhh in the back of my- my- my mind I feel that (.4) he's t- ta some degree retardet.

In contrast, an unmarked invitation does not propose a problem.

    10.002

    Dr. S: Now- (.6) uhh since (.4) you've (.1) been here and through this thing h:ow do you see R now (.4) Mrs C.

    Mrs. C: I guess I (.2) see him better since he here

9.001

Dr. S: Now that you've- we've been through all this I just
wanted know from you:::. (.4) how you see J at this
time.
(2.2)

Mrs. C: The same
(.7)

Dr. S: Which is?
(.5)

Mrs. C: Uhm she can't talk.....

The implications of marked and unmarked invitations are different
particularly with regard to what then follows in the sequence, the
delivery of diagnostic news.

Marked invitations can be considered as "suggestions or proposals
that require acceptance." These are presumptive moves on the part of
the clinician (based on either their own or other's findings) and this
presumption becomes evident when parents disagree with the clinician.
Instead of responding with their own description of the problem, the
recipients of the invitation may take exception to the presumption and
disagree.

22.007

04 Dr. N: It's obvious that uh- you- understand a fair amount (.2)
05 about what Charles' problem i[s.
06 Mrs. G: [y]is. (yeh).
.

.
16 Dr. N: S::o at this point there is a certain amount of
17 confusion.
18 (.2)
19 Mrs. G: Mm hmm
20 (.3)
21 Dr. N: in your mind probably as to what the problem really
22 is?
23 Mrs. G: Mm
24 Dr. N: .hh and we haven't really had a chance to hear from
25 you at all as to (.7) what you
26 f[eel the situation-
27 Mrs. G: [well I don't think] there's anything wrong with him.

To reject or disagree with the presumption may *prereject* the diagnosis and other recommendations the clinicians are about to present as well. Although the clinicians may go on to deliver the diagnosis, they have to deal with the disagreement in the immediate interactional situation.

In contrast, unmarked invitations, by inviting the parents to produce a complaint or problem description, enable the clinicians to confirm that a problem exists and to deliver their diagnosis. They thereby show an openness with respect to the formulation of the problem and align themselves with the parents' position (Maynard, 1991, p. 173).

Maynard goes on to ask what the significance of these two forms of invitation might be. On purely sequential and social organization terms, he says, perspective-display series work to achieve a delivery of diagnostic news, which is the purpose of the meeting. However, the marked invitation, when parents agree with the presumption, can move to the discussion of the problem immediately. If there is disagreement, then the disagreement is dealt with in ways that ask the recipients to modify their position while clinicians maintain their claims to expertise. That parents will maintain their disagreement is, of course, also a possibility.

In the unmarked invitations, alignment is also sought, but the route for attaining it is different. Once parents provide indications that there is a problem, the news that is delivered by clinicians is more confirmatory than presumptive. If parents do not provide a problem formulation in response to an unmarked invitation, clinicians can nevertheless proceed. But, because this is not an environment of disagreement, parents do not have to back down from a stated position, and the meeting can proceed without the disruptions associated with open disagreements.

Thus Maynard (1991, p. 187) concludes:

> [M]arked queries presumptively ask recipients for their view, immediately occasion talk that is relevant to the purpose of the interview, and, when parents are resistive to producing negative assessments of their child, entail conversational difficulty in the form of disagreement. Unmarked queries are less presumptive regarding the existence of a child's problems, allow an opportunity to topicalize matters other than that problem, and, when parents defy solicitations of complaints, allow disagreement to be avoided as a warranted movement is made to the presentation of clinical findings. . . . marked invitations seem most easily fitted to convergent views, while the unmarked variety facilitate dealing with both convergent and divergent perspectives.

A result of strategically employing these various procedures . . . is to maximize the potential for presenting clinical assessments as agreeing with recipient's perspectives or in a publicly affirmative and nonconflicting manner. This demonstrates participants' sensitivity to the interactional context of news delivery and receipt.

As this study shows, the close attention to the interaction in sessions where diagnostic news is presented revealed the use of different sequential forms in a PDS, specifically the marked and unmarked invitation. These forms are sensitive to the situation and the type of activity in which the parties are engaged. The analysis of interaction thereby reveals the presence and use of interactional structures that enable the parties to achieve or produce the work of the clinic. In this sense, interaction analysis reveals how the work of the clinic is organized.

It should be noted that in the discussion of these studies, we have carefully avoided formulations that employ the vocabularies and theoretical perspectives conventionally used in sociological studies of organizations, for example, roles, norms, status, control, authority, hierarchy, and so on, and any theoretical/explanatory schemas. The respecification of the problem of social order by ethnomethodology and conversation analysis argues instead for a focus on the ways in which practical actions in any setting are organized, in what ways members orient their actions to each other, within the practical constraints such actions produce. Social actions occur in a context, the context provided by prior and next actions, the presence of others, the formulations and reformulations of meanings, of what has been (or is about to be) done, and the setting's own accountable character, as found in what and how members orient to such matters.

In short, from the ethnomethodological perspective as incorporated in conversation analysis, settings and actions are mutually and inextricably interrelated. Social actions are "actions conducting-the-affairs-of-a-social-order" (Sharrock & Button, 1991, p. 171) and therefore inseparable from social order. The effort to pose social structure as an independent force constraining, affecting, influencing, or determining social action posits a theoretically conceived dichotomous relationship between matters that cannot be separated. Because this position is not compatible with either the ontological or epistemological position of ethnomethodology and conversation analysis, formulations concerning social structure (and its related conceptual vocabularies) are neither acceptable nor incorporatable, nor are proposals that the task of analysis is to find causal relationships between social structure and social actions. The task of ethnomethodology and conversation analysis, as we have shown, is to uncover, describe, and analyze the ways in which social order is ongoingly produced, achieved, and made recognizable in and through the practical actions of members of society. This task is *explicatory* rather than *explanatory* (Sharrock & Button, 1991, p. 167) and as such requires careful attention to the ways that members accomplish social actions/social order in and through their ordinary language usages in everyday interaction. Furthermore, as Sacks has demonstrated repeatedly in his lectures (1989, 1992), members provide for each other, in what they say, inference-rich material for making sense and achieving intelligibility in everyday life. The task of analysis is to show how this is accomplished, not to offer a constructive analytic theorist's account that seeks to explain everything in the interest of providing a broad, generalizing, interpretive gloss.

6. CONCLUSION

What has been presented here is not so much a field of study, though conversation analysis has aspects of a field in its examination of the organization of naturally occurring talk, but rather an approach and a method for studying social interaction, utilizable for a wide, unspecifiable range of social phenomena, that is, social actions, which enable the discovery of their forms, their structures, their machinery, their methodical procedures.

It is a method that has instructable features, a method that can be taught and learned, that can be demonstrated and that has achieved reproducible results.

As linguists and others have also turned to the examination of talk, there have been attempts, such as discourse analysis, to achieve more formal descriptions and to utilize the concepts and theories developed in linguistics. Conversation analysis is, however, distinguishable from discourse analysis (Levinson, 1983) in that discourse analysis tries to develop a set of basic categories or units of discourse, to find specific and delimited sets of unit acts, and to formulate rules concerning "well formed sequences of categories (coherent discourse) from ill-formed (incoherent discourses)." In general, by drawing methods and theories from theoretical linguistics, discourse analysis seems inappropriate for the study of the detailed particularities of conversation, which is, after all, an interactional production.

As part of the broad movement within sociology called ethnomethodology, conversation analysis has fulfilled many of the promises of ethnomethodology to be the study of the ways in which members ongoingly produce social order, focusing on the indexical and reflexive features of such production and on the pragmatic character of accounts, while at the same time refusing to present its findings and formulations in overly theoretical or abstract terms.

The growing body of studies (see especially Coulter, 1990, for an extended bibliography of several hundred studies) represents a significant accomplishment over three decades of research. It has been adopted as a method in various fields in addition to sociology, for example, anthropology (Moerman, 1988), communication research (Hopper, 1992), and social studies of science (Button, 1993); and has produced studies in the various fields and subfields of sociology, for example, medical sociology (Frankel, 1984, 1989, 1990; Heath, 1984, 1986; Ten Have,

1991), deviance and criminology (Maynard, 1984; Meehan, 1989; Watson, 1990), sociology of science and technology (Button, 1993), the sociology of children (Goodwin, 1990), as well as in basic studies of social interaction (represented in various collections: Atkinson & Heritage, 1984; Button & Lee, 1987; Psathas, 1979, 1990; Schenkein, 1978, among others). There is no "fixed agenda intrinsic to conversation analysis, any more than there is for ethnomethodology or, indeed, the discipline of sociology as a whole. . . . [It] represents a general approach to the analysis of social action which can be applied to an extremely varied array of topics and problems" (Heritage, 1984, p. 291).

It is hoped that this introductory overview will provide interested readers and researchers with an indication of the range and scope of inquiries conducted under the methodological auspices of conversation analysis. Other reviewers of the field have provided excellent and informative introductions as well (Goodwin & Heritage, 1990; Heritage, 1984, 1989; Zimmerman, 1988).

The study of talk-in-interaction brings more than a promise, because it has now achieved a demonstrable record of rigorous, systematic, replicable, and cumulative studies. It offers an answer to what Goffman had proposed was needed, namely, the study of interaction as a field in its own right, the study of "interaction in natural settings" (Goffman, 1967, p. 1); "the syntactical relations among the acts of different persons mutually present to one another" (Goffman, 1967, p. 2); the study of face-to-face interaction as a naturally bounded, analytically coherent field (Goffman, 1969, p. ix); and the "interaction order as a substantive domain in its own right" (Goffman, 1983, p. 2).

However, at the same time, it has respecified the phenomena in ways that differ from Goffman's formulations. These studies have thereby contributed to reformulations that have analytic coherence and methodological rigor. They have also uncovered an order of phenomena that Goffman never considered and that his methods of observation prevented him from discerning.

It is clear, as Schegloff (1988, p. 91) has said, that although he and Sacks had studied with Goffman, "appreciated his achievement and meant [their] own efforts to build on it in some respects," the position that Goffman came to (in *Forms of Talk*, 1981a, and "The Interaction Order," 1983) is "no longer the way to work in this area." Schegloff's (1988, p. 131) claim is that conversation analysis is "the study of syntactical relations between acts, a sociology of interaction as a potentially rigorous discipline."

Following Schegloff's lead, I will say it most emphatically—that "different way" is conversation analysis, the study of talk-in-interaction.

APPENDIX:
TRANSCRIPTION SYMBOLS

With a few exceptions, the transcription symbols are those developed by Gail Jefferson to capture those phenomena relevant to the organization of conversation. They specifically note the location of silence, onset of speech, overlapped speech, and phenomena relevant to interactional units such as turns, turn transitions, and turn completions. Although the system obviously does not capture all the distinctions that can be made in the analysis of talk, it aims to provide the reader with a description of those features most relevant to the analysis of the organization of talk-in-interaction.

Researchers do not use all of the symbols since they may be interested in different aspects of interaction, and some add new symbols in order to describe those phenomena to which their study may be oriented. Nevertheless, most researchers within the conversation analysis tradition have found the basic aspects of this notation system both useful and adequate.

Certain conventions used in the presentation of research reports are also included here.

The major sources relied upon for this listing are Sacks, Schegloff, and Jefferson (1974); Psathas (1979); Goodwin (1981); Atkinson and Heritage (1984); and Psathas and Anderson (1990). Some variations in these several sources are due to the inability of type fonts or word-processing programs to handle particular symbols, and some are due to preferences of different transcribers for particular symbols to represent speech phenomena.

I. Sequencing

1. SIMULTANEOUS UTTERANCES

Utterances starting up simultaneously are linked together with double left-hand brackets.

    Tom: [[I used to smoke a lot when I was young
    Bob: [[I used to smoke Camels

2. OVERLAP

A: Beginning of overlap

When utterances overlap but do not start up simultaneously, the point at which overlap begins is marked by a single left-hand bracket.

> Tom: I used to smoke [a lot
> Bob: [he thinks he's real tough

An alternative notation for beginning of overlap is to use double oblique markers to indicate the point at which the overlap begins.

> V: Th'guy says tuh me- .hh my son// dided.
> M: Wuhjeh do:.

A multiple-overlapped utterance is followed, in serial order, by the talk that overlaps it. Thus C's "Vi:c" (below) occurs simultaneously with V's "left"; and C's "Victuh" with V's "hallway."

> V: I//left my garbage pail in iz//hallway
> C: Vi:c
> C: Victuh,

B. End of Overlap
The point where overlapping utterances stop overlapping is marked with a single right-hand bracket.

> Tom: I used to smoke [a lot] more than this
> Bob: [I see]

An alternative notation for end of overlap is an asterisk to indicate the point at which two overlapping or simultaneously started utterances end, if they end simultaneously, or the point at which one of them ends in the course of another or the point at which one utterance component ends vis-à-vis another.

> M: [[I mean no no n'no*
> V: [[P't it back up*
> M: [[Jim? wasn' home* uh what.
> V: [[Y'know:w?*

3. LATCHING OR CONTIGUOUS UTTERANCES

Equal signs indicate latching (i.e., no interval between the end of a prior and the start of a next part of talk).

A. Latching with change of speakers

```
Tom:   I used to smoke a lot=
Bob:   =He thinks he's real tough
```

B. Latching by more than one speaker
Two speakers begin simultaneously and with no interval between
their start and the end of the last speaker's talk.

```
Tom:   I used to smoke a lot=
Bob:   =[[He thinks he's real tough
Ann:   =[[So did I
```

C. Latching at the end of overlapped speech
Two utterances end simultaneously and are latched onto by a next.

```
Tom:   I used to smoke [a lot]=
Bob:                   [I see ]
Ann:   =So did I
```

D. Latching within the same speaker's talk

```
V:     well my son did it=I'm gladjer son didn't get hurt...
```

E. Latching as a transcription convenience
When a speaker's lengthy utterance is broken up arbitrarily for purposes of presentation, especially when overlap occurs, the equals
sign is used to indicate continuity in the same speaker's utterance.

```
V:     my wif//caught d'ki:d,=
R:     yeh
V:     =lightin a fiyuh in Perry's cellar
```

```
Tom:   I used to smoke [a lot more than this=
Bob:                   [you used to smoke
Tom:   =but I never inhaled the smoke
```

II. Timed Intervals, Within and Between Utterances

Silences, pauses, and gaps, as intervals in the stream of talk, are
timed in tenths of a second and noted where they occur.

1. NUMBERS IN PARENTHESES

The number indicates in seconds and tenths of a second the length of
an interval.

Lil: When I was (0.6) oh nine or ten
(0.4)
Joe: Are you talking to me?

A. One alternative is to use dashes within parentheses.
Each dash is a tenth of a second; each full second is marked with a plus sign.

J: How's uh, (---------+-----) Jimmy

B. A second alternative is the use of plus markers within parentheses. Each plus mark is one tenth of a second; each full second may be marked by a space.

J: How's uh, (++++++++++ +++++) Jimmy

2. UNTIMED MICRO-INTERVALS

More or less than a tenth of a second is indicated by a dot within parentheses.

J: barges are struck (.) stuck that is

3. UNTIMED INTERVALS OF LONGER LENGTH

If timing is not achieved, a pause, silence, or gap may be noted as untimed. Pause is generally noted within a speaker's turn and gap as occurring between turns.

J: who all is there.
K: oh, Marcia and Judy stopped by
((gap))
J: who else
K: oh, what's his name ((pause)) Tom.
J: oh.

III. Characteristics of Speech Production

Punctuation marks are used to describe characteristics of speech production. They are not to be interpreted as referring to grammatical units.

1. SOUND STRETCH

A colon indicates that the prior sound is prolonged. Multiple colons indicate a more prolonged sound.

V: So dih gu:y sez
M: I ju::ss can't come
T: I'm so::: sorry re:::ally I am

2. CUT-OFF

A single dash indicates a cut-off of the prior word or sound (i.e., a noticeable and abrupt termination).

C: Th' U:sac- uh:, sprint car dr- dirt track.........

3. INTONATION

A. A period indicates a stopping fall in tone.

F: So with every (.) economic failure. (0.5) they turn (0.5)
      more viciously. (0.5) on the local authorities.

B. A comma indicates a continuing intonation, for example, the kind of falling-rising contour one finds after items in a list.

A: There was a bear, a cat, enna dog.

C. Question mark indicates a rising intonation. Question mark/comma indicates rising intonation weaker than that indicated by a question mark/period.

V: A do:g? enna cat is different.
P: Yih ever take'er out again?,

D. Marked rising and falling shifts in intonation are indicated by upward and downward pointing arrows immediately prior to the rise or fall.

T: I am however (0.2) very fortunate (0.4) in having (0.6)
      a ↑ marvelous deputy.

E. Exclamation point indicates an animated tone.

C: An that! so what he sez.

4. EMPHASIS

Emphasis is indicated by italics or underscoring. The larger the letters, the greater the relative stress.

Ann: It happens to be.
Ben: Its not either yours it's <u>MINE</u>
V: I sex y'know <u>WHY</u>, becawss <u>look</u>

5. PITCH

The relationship between emphasis and prolongation (stretch) indicate pitch change (or nonchange) in the course of a word.

A. Word stressed but with no change in pitch.
To indicate stress (and here stretching as well), the stress-mark is placed on the first letter of the stressed syllable. Of course, if the stressing is greater, then the underscore is longer.

J: it's only a venee:r though,

B. Pitch drop

J: it's only a venee:r though,

To indicate pitch-drop, the underscore should be placed at the vowel immediately preceding the colon. Again, for more pronounced emphasis, the underscore is longer.

J: it's only venee:r though,

The idea is not to have the colon underscored and an immediately preceding vowel underscored.

C. Pitch rise
To indicate pitch rise, the stress is marked upon the prolongation.

J: it's only venee::r though,

If the rise occurs somewhere in the course of a prolongation, that can be shown as follows:

J: it's only a venee:::::r though,

And one can show rising and falling

J: it's only a venee::::::r though,

6. VOLUME

A. Loudness
Upper-case letters are used to indicate increased volume.

> V: In it dint fall OUT!

B. Softness
A degree sign is used to show a passage of talk that has a noticeably lower volume then the surrounding talk.

> J: An' how are you feeling? (0.4) °these days,°

IV. Aspiration—Audible Inhalation and Exhalation

An h or series of h's is used to mark an out-breath unless a dot precedes the h's, in which case an in-breath is indicated.

1. OUT-BREATH

> J: I'm not sure hh- who it belongs to

2. IN-BREATH

> M: .hhh Okay, thank you Mister Hanys'n=

Plosive aspiration as in laughter, breathlessness, or crying is indicated by placing the h in parentheses.

> Pam: An th(hh)sis for you hhh
> Gene: So that shook up the old (h)house(h)hold up fer
>   a(h)whil(h)le heh
> Joyce: ehh [hhhhhhh!
> C: [oh(hh)h hah huh!

V. Transcriptionist Doubt

Other than the timings of intervals and inserted aspirations, items enclosed within single parentheses are in doubt.

> Ted: I ('spose I'm not)
> (Ben): We al (t-)

Sometimes, multiple possibilities are indicated.

(spoke to Mark)
Ted: I ('spose I'm not)

When single parentheses are empty, no hearing could be achieved for the talk or item in question.

Todd: My ( ) catching
( ):   In my highest ( )

On occasion, nonsense syllables are provided in an attempt to capture something of the produced sounds.

R: (Y' cattuh moo)

VI. Verbal Descriptions

Double parentheses are used to enclose a description of some phenomenon with which the transcriptionist does not want to contend. These may be vocalizations that are not easily spelled, details of the conversational scene, or various characterizations of the talk.

Tom: I used to ((cough)) smoke a lot
Bob: ((sniffle)) He thinks he's tough
Ann: ((snorts))

Jan: This is just delicious
        ((telephone rings))
Kim: I'll get it

Ron: ((in falsetto)) I can do it now
Max: ((whispered)) He'll never do it

VII. Presentation Conventions

1. TO CALL ATTENTION OF READER

Arrows or dots in the left-hand margin of the transcript may be used to call the reader's attention to particular parts of the transcript. The author will inform the reader of the significance of the referent of the arrow (or dot) by discussing it in the text.

Don: If I had the money I'd get one for her
→ Sam: And one for your mother too I'll bet

Don: I like the blue one very much
• Sam: An I'll bet your wife would like it

2. ELLIPSES

A. Horizontal ellipses indicate that an utterance is partially reported, that is, parts of the same speaker's utterance are omitted

J: hhh (0.4) hhh <u>we</u> just want to get ....

B. Vertical ellipses indicate that intervening turns at talk have been omitted.

12. Bob: Well I always say give it your all
.
.
.
.
19. Bob: I always give it everything

3. NUMBERING OF LINES OR UTTERANCE PARTS

Numbering in a transcript is arbitrarily done for convenience or reference. Line numbers are not intended to be measures of timing or number of turns or utterances. Silences between talk may also receive line numbers.

11. Tim: Nice hand Chris:.
12. (0.4)
13. Jim: Th'ts a nice ha:nd.

REFERENCES

Atkinson, J. M. (1984). *Our master's voices*. London: Methuen.

Atkinson, J. M., & Drew, P. (1979). *Order in court: The organization of verbal interaction in judicial settings*. Atlantic Highlands, NJ: Humanities Press.

Atkinson, J. M., & Heritage, J. C. (1984). *Structures of social action: Studies in conversation analysis*. Cambridge, UK: Cambridge University Press.

Bales, R. F. (1950). *Interaction process analysis*. Cambridge, MA: Addison-Wesley.

Barker, R. G. (1951). *One boy's day: A specimen record of behavior*. New York: Harper.

Barker, R. G., & Wright, H. F. (1955). *Midwest and its children*. Evanston, IL: Row, Peterson.

Bateson, G. (1955). A theory of play and fantasy. In *Psychiatric research reports: Vol. 2. Approaches to the study of human personality* (pp. 39-51). Washington, DC: American Psychiatric Association.

Bateson, G. (1972). *Steps to an ecology of mind: Collected essays in anthropology, psychiatry, evolution, and epistemology*. San Francisco: Chandler.

Benson, D., & Hughes, J. (1991). Method: Evidence and inference—Evidence and inference for ethnomethodology. In G. Button (Ed.), *Ethnomethodology and the human sciences* (pp. 109-136). Cambridge, UK: Cambridge University Press.

Birdwhistell, R. L. (1952). *Introduction to kinesics*. Washington, DC: Foreign Service Institute.

Birdwhistell, R. L. (1970). *Kinesics and context: Essays on body motion*. Philadelphia: University of Pennsylvania Press.

Boden, D., & Zimmerman, D. H. (Eds.). (1991). *Talk and social structure: Studies in ethnomethodology and conversation analysis*. Cambridge, UK: Polity Press.

Button, G. (1987). Moving out of closings. In G. Button & J.R.E. Lee (Eds.), *Talk and social organization* (pp. 101-151). Clevedon, UK: Multilingual Matters.

Button, G. (1990). On varieties of closings. In G. Psathas (Ed.), *Interaction competence* (pp. 93-147). Washington, DC: University Press of America.

Button, G. (Ed.). (1993). *Technology in working order*. London & New York: Routledge.

Button, G., & Lee, J.R.E. (Eds.). (1987). *Talk and social organization*. Clevedon, UK: Multilingual Matters.

Cicourel, A. V. (1964). *Method and measurement in sociology*. New York: Free Press.

Clayman, S. (1988, October). Displaying neutrality in television news interview. *Social Problems, 34*(4), 474-492.

Coulter, J. (1983). Contingent and a priori structures in sequential analysis. *Human Studies, 6*(4), 361-376.

Coulter, J. (Ed.). (1990). *Ethnomethodological sociology*. Aldershot, UK, & Brookfield, VT: Edward Elgar.

Davidson, J. A. (1990). Modifications of invitations, offers and rejections. In G. Psathas (Ed.), *Interaction competence*. Washington, DC: University Press of America.

Frake, C. A. (1964). Notes on queries in ethnography. In A. K. Romney & R. G. D'Andrade (Eds.), Transcultural studies in cognition [Special issue, part 2]. *The American Anthropologist, 66*, 132-145.

Frankel, R. (1984). From sentence to sequence: Understanding the medical encounter through micro-interactional analysis. *Discourse Processes, 7*, 135-170.

79

Frankel, R. (1989). Microanalysis and the medical encounter. In D. T. Helm et al. (Eds.), *The interactional order: New directions in the study of social order* (pp. 21-49). New York: Irvington.

Frankel, R. (1990). Talking in interviews: A dispreference for patient-initiated questions in physician-patient encounters. In G. Psathas (Ed.), *Interaction competence* (pp. 231-264). Washington, DC: University Press of America.

Garfinkel, H., & Sacks, H. (1970). On formal structures of practical actions. In J. C. McKinney & E. A. Tiryakian (Eds.), *Theoretical sociology* (pp. 338-366). New York: Appleton-Century-Crofts.

Goffman, E. (1959). *The presentation of self in everyday life.* Garden City, NY: Doubleday Anchor.

Goffman, E. (1963). *Behavior in public places.* New York: Free Press.

Goffman, E. (1967). *Interaction ritual: Essays on face-to-face behavior.* New York: Doubleday Anchor.

Goffman, E. (1969). *Strategic interaction.* Philadelphia: University of Pennsylvania Press.

Goffman, E. (1971). *Relations in public.* New York: Basic Books.

Goffman, E. (1981a). *Forms of talk.* Philadelphia: University of Pennsylvania Press.

Goffman, E. (1981b). Radio talk. In E. Goffman, *Forms of talk* (pp. 197-327). Philadelphia: University of Pennsylvania Press.

Goffman, E. (1983). The interaction order. *American Sociological Review, 48,* 1-17.

Goodenough, W. (1957). Cultural anthropology and linguistics. In P. L. Garvin (Ed.), *Monograph series on languages and linguistics* (No. 9) (pp. 167-173). Washington, DC: Institute of Languages and Linguistics.

Goodwin, C. (1981). *Conversational organization: Interaction between speakers and hearers.* New York: Academic Press.

Goodwin, C. (1984). Notes on story structure and the organization of participation. In J. M. Atkinson & J. Heritage (Eds.), *Structures of social action: Studies in conversation analysis* (pp. 225-246). Cambridge, UK: Cambridge University Press.

Goodwin, C., & Heritage, J. (1990). Conversation analysis. *Annual Review of Anthropology, 19,* 283-307.

Goodwin, M. H. (1990). *He-said-she-said: Talk as social organization among black children.* Bloomington & Indianapolis: Indiana University Press.

Gumperz, J. J., & Hymes, D. (Eds.). (1964). The ethnography of communication [Special issue, part 2]. *The American Anthropologist, 66.*

Hammel, E. A. (Ed.). (1965). Formal semantic analysis [Special issue, part 2]. *The American Anthropologist, 67*(5).

Heath, C. (1984). Talk and recipiency: Sequential organization in speech and body movment. In J. M. Atkinson & J. Heritage (Eds.), *Structures of social action: Studies in conversation analysis* (pp. 247-265). Cambridge, UK: Cambridge University Press.

Heath, C. (1986). *Body movement and speech in medical interaction.* Cambridge, UK: Cambridge University Press.

Heritage, J. (1984). Conversation analysis. In J. Heritage, *Garfinkel and ethnomethodology.* Cambridge, UK: Polity Press.

Heritage, J. (1989). Current developments in conversation analysis. In D. Roger & P. Bull (Eds.), *Conversation: An interdisciplinary perspective* (pp. 21-47). Clevedon, UK: Multilingual Matters.

Heritage, J., & Greatbatch, D. (1991). On the institutional character of institutional talk: The case of news interviews. In D. Boden & D. H. Zimmerman (Eds.), *Talk and social structure* (pp. 93-136). Cambridge, UK: Polity Press.

Hopper, R. (1992). *Telephone conversation*. Bloomington & Indianapolis: Indiana University Press.

Hymes, D. (1964). Introduction. In J. J. Gumperz & D. Hymes (Eds.), The ethnography of communication [Special issue, part 2]. *The American Anthropologist, 66*(6).

Jefferson, G. (1978). Sequential aspects of storytelling in conversation. In J. Schenkein (Ed.), *Studies in the organization of conversational interaction* (pp. 219-248). New York: Academic Press.

Jefferson, G. (1990). List construction as a task and resource. In G. Psathas (Ed.), *Interaction competence*. Washington, DC: University Press of America.

Levinson, S. C. (1983). Conversational structure. In S. C. Levinson, *Pragmatics* (pp. 284-370). Cambridge, UK: Cambridge University Press.

Maynard, D. (1984). *Inside plea bargaining: The language of negotiation*. New York & London: Plenum.

Maynard, D. (1991). The perspective-display series and the delivery and receipt of diagnostic news. In D. Boden & D. H. Zimmerman (Eds.), *Talk and social structure* (pp. 164-192). Cambridge, UK: Polity Press.

Meehan, A. J. (1989). Assessing the "policeworthiness" of citizen complaints to the police. In D. T. Helm, W. T. Anderson, A. J. Meehan, & A. W. Rawls (Eds.), *The interactional order: New directions in the study of social order* (pp. 16-20). New York: Irvington.

Merleau-Ponty, M. (1968). *The phenomenology of perception*. London: Routledge & Kegan Paul.

Moerman, M. (1988). *Talking culture: Ethnography and conversation analysis*. Philadelphia: University of Pennsylvania Press.

Pittenger, R. E., Hockett, C. F., & Danehy, J. J. (1960). *The first five minutes*. Ithaca, NY: P. Martineau.

Pollner, M. (1979). Explicative transactions: Making and managing meaning in traffic court. In G. Psathas (Ed.), *Everyday language: Studies in ethnomethodology* (pp. 227-255). New York: Irvington.

Pomerantz, A. (1978). Compliment responses: Notes on the co-operation of multiple constraints. In J. Schenkein (Ed.), *Studies in the organization of conversational interaction* (pp. 79-112). New York: Academic Press.

Psathas, G. (Ed.). (1979). *Everyday language: Studies in ethnomethodology*. New York: Irvington.

Psathas, G. (1986a, April-August). The organization of directions in interaction. *Word, 37*(1-2), 83-91.

Psathas, G. (1986b). Some sequential structures in direction-giving. *Human Studies, 9*(2-3), 231-246.

Psathas, G. (Ed.). (1990). *Interaction competence*. Washington, DC: University Press of America.

Psathas, G. (1991). The structure of direction-giving in interaction. In D. Boden & D. H. Zimmerman (Eds.), *Talk and social structure* (pp. 196-216). Cambridge, UK: Polity Press.

Psathas, G. (1992, April). *Discovering the structure of an organization.* Paper presented at meetings of the Eastern Sociological Society, Washington, DC.

Psathas, G., & Anderson, W. T. (1990, January). The "practices" of transcription in conversation analysis. *Semiotica, 78*(12), 75-99.

Reusch, J., & Bateson, G. (1951). *Communication: The social matrix of psychiatry.* New York: Norton.

Romney, A. K., & D'Andrade, R. G. (Eds.). (1964). Transcultural studies in cognition [Special issue, part 2]. *The American Anthropologist, 66*(3).

Sacks, H. (1964-72). Lectures, unpublished mimeos (G. Jefferson, Ed.). (1964-68: University of California, Los Angeles; 1968-72: University of California, Irvine)

Sacks, H. (1989). Lectures, 1964-65 (G. Jefferson, Ed.; E. A. Schegloff, Introduction/memoir). *Human Studies, 12*(3-4).

Sacks, H. (1992). *Lectures on conversation* (Vols. 1 & 2; G. Jefferson, Ed.; E. A. Schegloff, Introduction). Oxford, UK, & Cambridge, MA: Blackwell.

Sacks, H., Schegloff, E. A., & Jefferson, G. (1974). A simplest systematics for the organization of turn-taking for conversation. *Language, 50*(4), 696-735. (Also in J. Schenkein. (Ed.). (1978). *Studies in the organization of conversational interaction* (pp. 7-56). New York: Academic Press.)

Schegloff, E. A. (1968). Sequencing in conversational openings. *The American Anthropologist, 70*(6), 1075-1095. (Also in J. J. Gumperz & D. Hymes (Eds.). (1972). *Directions in sociologinuistics: The ethnography of communication* (pp. 346-380). New York: Holt, Rinehart & Winston.)

Schegloff, E. A. (1979). Identification and recognition in telephone conversation openings. In G. Psathas (Ed.), *Everyday language: Studies in ethnomethodology.* New York: Irvington.

Schegloff, E. A. (1986). The routine as achievement. *Human Studies, 9*(2-3), 111-151.

Schegloff, E. A. (1988). Goffman and the analysis of conversation. In P. Drew & A. Wootton (Eds.), *Erving Goffman: Exploring the interaction order* (pp. 89-135). Cambridge, UK: Polity Press.

Schegloff, E. A., Jefferson, G., & Sacks, H. (1977). The preference for self-correction in the organization of repair in conversation. *Language, 53*, 361-382. (Also in G. Psathas. (Ed.). (1990). *Interaction competence* (pp. 31-62). Washington, DC: University Press of America.)

Schegloff, E. A., & Sacks, H. (1973). Opening up closings. *Semiotica, 7*, 289-327. (Also in R. Turner. (Ed.). (1974). *Ethnomethodology* (pp. 233-264). Harmondsworth, UK, & Baltimore, MD: Penguin.)

Schenkein, J. (Ed.). (1978). *Studies in the organization of conversational interaction.* New York: Academic Press.

Sharrock, W. W., & Button, G. (1991). The social actor: Social action in real time. In G. Button (Ed.), *Ethnomethodology and the human sciences* (pp. 137-175). Cambridge, UK: Cambridge University Press.

Soskin, W., & John, V. (1963). The study of spontaneous talk. In R. G. Barker (Ed.), *The stream of behavior* (pp. 228-281). New York: Appleton- Century-Crofts.

Sturtevant, W. C. (1964). Studies in ethnoscience. In A. K. Romney & R. G. D'Andrade (Eds.), Transcultural studies in cognition [Special issue, part 2]. *The American Anthropologist, 66*(3), 99-131.

Ten Have, P. (1991). Talk and institution: A reconsideration of the "asymmetry" of doctor-patient interaction. In D. Boden & D. H. Zimmerman (Eds.), *Talk and social structure* (pp. 138-163). Cambridge, UK: Polity Press.

Turner, R. (Ed.). (1974). *Ethnomethodology*. Harmondsworth, UK, & Baltimore, MD: Penguin.

Watson, D. R. (1990). Some features of the elicitation of confessions in murder interrogations. In G. Psathas (Ed.), *Interaction competence* (pp. 263-296). Washington, DC: University Press of America.

Whalen, J. (1994). A technology of order production: Computer-aided dispatch in public safety communications. In P. ten Have & G. Psathas (Eds.), *Situated order: Studies in the social organization of talk and embodied activities*. Washington, DC: University Press of America.

Zimmerman, D. H. (1988). On conversation: The conversation analytic perspective (pp. 406-432) (Communication Yearbook 11). Newbury Park, CA: Sage.

Zimmerman, D. H. (1992). Achieving context: Openings in emergency calls. In G. Watson & R. Seiler (Eds.), *Text in context: Contributions to ethnomethodology*. Newbury Park, CA: Sage.

Additional References

Button, G. (Ed.). (1991). *Ethnomethodology and the human sciences*. Cambridge, UK: Cambridge University Press.

Garfinkel, H. (1967). *Studies in ethnomethodology*. Englewood Cliffs, NJ: Prentice-Hall. (Paperback edition. 1984. *Studies in ethnomethodology*. Cambridge, UK: Polity Press)

Garfinkel, H. (1988). Evidence for locally produced, naturally accountable phenomena of order: An announcemnt of studies. *Sociological Theory, 6*, 103-109.

Goffman, E. (1961). *Encounters: Two studies in the sociology of interaction*. Indianapolis: Bobbs-Merrill.

Goodwin, C. (1979). The interactive construction of a sentence in natural conversation. In G. Psathas (Ed.), *Everyday language: Studies in ethnomethodology* (pp. 97-121). New York: Irvington.

Greatbatch, D. (1988). A turn-taking system for British news interviews. *Language in Society, 17*, 401-430.

Helm, D. T., Anderson, W. T., Meehan, A. J., & Rawls, A. W. (Eds.). (1989). *The interactional order: New directions in the study of social order*. New York: Irvington.

Heritage, J. C., Clayman, S. E., & Zimmerman, D. H. (1988). Discourse and message analysis: The micro-structure of mass media messages. In R. Hawkins, S. Pingree, & J. Weimann (Eds.), *Advancing communication science: Merging mass and interpersonal processes* (pp. 77-109) (Sage Annual Reviews of Communication Research, Vol. 16). Newbury Park, CA: Sage.

Jefferson, G. (1979). A technique for inviting laughter and its subsequent acceptance/declination. In G. Psathas (Ed.), *Everyday language: Studies in ethnomethodology*. New York: Irvington.

84

Jefferson, G., Sacks, H., & Schegloff, E. A. (1986). On laughter in the pursuit of intimacy. In G. Button & J.R.E. Lee (Eds.), *Talk and social organization* (pp. 152-205). Clevedon, UK: Multilingual Matters.

Lee, J.R.E. (1986). Prologue: Talking organization. In G. Button & J.R.E. Lee (Eds.), *Talk and social organization* (pp. 19-53). Clevedon, UK: Multilingual Matters.

Pomerantz, A. (1984). Agreeing and disagreeing with assessments: Some features of preferred/dispreferred turn shapes. In J. M. Atkinson & J. C. Heritage (Eds.), *Structures of social action: Studies in conversation analysis* (pp. 57-101). Cambridge, UK: Cambridge University Press.

Pomerantz, A. (1987). Descriptions in legal settings. In G. Button & J.R.E. Lee (Eds.), *Talk and social organization* (pp. 226-243). Clevedon, UK: Multilingual Matters.

Psathas, G. (1992, August). *Calls and work: Talk and social structure and studies of work.* Paper presented at meetings of the International Institute for Ethnomethodology and Conversation Analysis, Bentley College, Waltham, MA.

Sacks, H. (1967). The search for help: No one to turn to. In E. S. Schneidman (Ed.), *Essays in self destruction* (pp. 203-223). New York: Science House.

Sacks, H. (1972). An initial investigation of the usability of conversational data for doing sociology. In D. N. Sudnow (Ed.), *Studies in social interaction* (pp. 31-74). New York: Free Press.

Sacks, H. (1972). On the analyzability of stories by children. In J. J. Gumperz & D. Hymes (Eds.), *Directions in sociolinguistics: The ethnography of communication* (pp. 325-345). New York: Holt, Rinehart & Winston. (Reprinted in R. Turner. (Ed.). (1974). *Ethnomethodology* (pp. 216-232). Harmondsworth, UK, & Baltimore, MD: Penguin)

Sacks, H. (1984). Lecture 1971, University of California, Irvine. Incorporated in Notes on methodology. In J. M. Atkinson & J. Heritage (Eds.), *Structures of social action: Studies in conversation analysis* (pp. 21-27). Cambridge, UK: Cambridge University Press.

Sudnow, D. (Ed.). (1972). *Studies in social interaction.* New York: Free Press.

Ten Have, P., & Psathas, G. (Eds.). (1994). *Situated order: Studies in the social organization of talk and embodied activities.* Washington, DC: University Press of America.

Watson, G., & Seiler, R. M. (Eds.). (1992). *Text in context: Contributions to ethnomethodology.* Newbury Park, CA: Sage.

Whalen, J. (1992). Conversation analysis. In E. F. Borgatta (Ed.), *Encyclopedia of sociology* (pp. 303-310). New York: Macmillan.

Whalen, M. R., & Zimmerman, D. H. (1987). Sequential and institutional contexts in calls for help. *Social Psychology Quarterly, 50,* 172-185.

Zimmerman, D. H. (1994). The interactional organization of calls for emergency assistance. In P. Drew & J. Heritage (Eds.), *Talk at work.* Cambridge, UK: Cambridge University Press.

ABOUT THE AUTHOR

GEORGE PSATHAS is Professor of Sociology at Boston University, where he has taught since 1968. He received his graduate degrees at the University of Michigan (M.A.) and Yale (Ph.D). He has taught and lectured on ethnomethodology and conversation analysis at universities and international conferences in Aberdeen, Ankara, Athens, Berlin, Calgary, Kyoto, London, Oxford, Paris, Tokyo, Toronto, and many American centers. He has offered courses on conversation analysis at Boston University for many years and at Doshisha University in Kyoto, Japan, in 1989. His recent works are *Interaction Competence* (1990), an edited collection of papers on interaction analysis copublished by the International Institute for Ethnomethodology and Conversation Analysis and the University Press of America, and *Phenomenology and Sociology: Theory and Research* (1989). He is the founder and editor-in-chief (since 1978) of the international quarterly journal, *Human Studies: A Journal for Philosophy and the Social Sciences.*